MIKE NELSON'S
MOVIE
MEGACHEESE

Michael J. Nelson

HarperEntertainment
An Imprint of HarperCollins*Publishers*

Some of this material appeared in slightly different form in *Home Theater* and *Entertainment@Home* magazines.

HarperCollins books may be purchased for educational, business, or sales promotional use. For information please write: Special Markets Department, HarperCollins Publishers Inc., 10 East 53rd Street, New York, NY 10022.

FIRST EDITION

Designed by Helene Berinsky

Library of Congress Cataloging-in-Publication Data has been applied for.

ISBN 0-380-81467-6

00 01 02 03 04 ❖/RRD 10 9 8 7 6 5 4 3 2

For the very real suffering they have endured,
I dedicate this book to the countless millions
of courageous victims who have witnessed the
feature film version of Lost in Space.

You will heal.

ACKNOWLEDGMENTS

There are many people I'd like to thank, even if they would rather not be indicted for their complicity in the creation of this book. Let me reassure all of you—there might be some uncomfortable questions, yes. *Why is this guy thanking you? How do you know him? Did he hurt you?* But most probably, it will pass without notice.

Bridget: Thanks and love. There will be other, less silly books in which to thank you properly.

Boys: I love you—now go to bed.

Many thanks to Tom Dupree at HarperCollins, for your talents, and for making this a great experience. Though, really—you'll never get me to believe that it's an *hour later* in New York?! What sense does that make? Thanks also to your wonderful assistant, Kelly Notaras.

Thanks to Tony Loew for his great photography and Russell Gordon for the art direction. You should know, you are the only men I've ever let cover me in popcorn.

To Kevin, Bill, Paul, Mary Jo, Patrick, Beez, Brad, Jim, Tim, Barb, Jeff M., Jeff S., Frank, Andrea, Trace, Joel, Peter, Parker, Jann, Ellie, Alex, Mike D., Dave S., Josh,

Acknowledgments

Heidi, Sarah, and all the folks at MST: Thanks for your friendship and for making me laugh 458,345 times (I counted).

To Bob, Dave, and Andy: As Kevin Tighe says, "I know you."

Thanks to the good folks at *Home Theater* magazine.

CONTENTS

INTRODUCTION

This book may not be as ambitious or exhaustive as *The Story of Philosophy,* or even *CorelDRAW 7 for Dummies.* But it does seek to answer one important question: What's the name of that one Carrot Top movie? The extent to which the writer succeeds in answering that question must, of course, be judged by the reader. I can only tell you that Mr. Top's film had the effect of numbing the memory of nearly everyone who saw it, rendering them useless for my research. Trips to the video store left me frustrated, for a man named Bob Kurtzwell checked out the tape in January of '99 and as of June had yet to return it. All the clerks I spoke with seemed unconcerned. Several months and tens of dollars later, I was able to obtain a copy and view it at my leisure for several days, and yet I, too, *retain no concrete memory of its content or title!*

Problems such as these are typical of those encountered when viewing bad films, and that point raises another question: Why do it at all? Certainly there are other things to write about. Why not write about architecture, or cats? Perhaps one could drop writing altogether and work at the airport? There are also many good positions available in retail; why not work at Target, or become a buyer for Neiman Marcus? These questions have plagued many writers over countless thousands of years. I can only tell you that for me, not writing about bad movies is not an option. Or rather, not *not* writing about bad movies isn't *not* an option. I guess what I'm saying is that not failing to not not write about bad movies isn't not a lack of being an option.

People have asked me if I hold to a unifying theory that informs my writing on cinema. In the past I've told them that I simply judge a movie on its success or failure in representing the perceived point of view of the filmmaker, but now I realize that I was just saying something to get rid of them. What I really believe is that a film should be judged on how well it comes off when compared with the Patrick Swayze film *Road House*. For *Road House* is the single finest American film. Certainly it stinks, but I believe the filmmakers meant it to, and succeeded grandly.

Therefore, films not containing poor performances by Patrick Swayze or Kevin Tighe will be judged harshly. Those that lack Ben Gazzara as their evil villain will be roundly castigated. There's no excuse for not telling the story of a legendary bouncer who finds love and confronts his demons at a small bar just outside Kansas City. And while adherence to a Road Housian standard certainly should be a requirement for every film, it needn't be the *only* requirement. A film should lack any image that could, whether by intent or negligence on the part of the filmmaker, seem to represent Adam Sandler. Every director should also take extreme precautions not to do a film based on the Irwin Allen series *Lost in Space*. It may seem unfathomable to you and me that this would even be considered, and yet *it actually happened.* Human beings got together and expended large amounts of energy to do just that! It should never be allowed to happen again.

So subjective is the process of reviewing movies that some readers will find themselves disagreeing with me on many points. For instance, while I thought that *Batman & Robin* roundly "sucked," others may think that it "eats," still others that it "bites" or "completely blows," and some might even hold that it "totally munches." I myself might even change my opinion over time, after seeing a film twice or looking at it from a different perspective. Whereas at one time I found *Waterworld* to be about as exciting as waiting for bread to toast, I now consider it to be nauseating and revolting. Quite a turnabout!

As you read these essays on bad cinema, you may feel compelled to go out on your own and "rent a couple of stinkers" or "throw back a few baddies." Certainly, do. But please be careful and take precautions. Always watch with a friend. (I don't have this luxury because I have one, maybe two friends, tops, and they know better.) Wear eye protection to avoid dangerous flying shards of Keanu Reeves. Some might even prefer to use safety glasses with a tint dark enough to avoid seeing the screen at all. Watch in short increments if fatigue sets in—no more than thirteen minutes of David Spade at a time. (I once lost track of time and found that I had viewed an entire Jean-Claude Van Damme film in one sitting! I felt as though I had been beaten by a sack filled with small cans of shoe polish, and that the contents of my skull had been removed and replaced with candied yams.) Drink plenty of liquids and stock up on Brazil nuts. Their bitterness makes them completely inedible, but they are the perfect size for throwing at the screen.

Try to enjoy movies that fit your personality. If you're into surfing and water sports, you might enjoy *Point Break*, with Keanu Reeves and Patrick Swayze. Dog lovers will certainly want to watch Jim Belushi's outlandish antics in the smash hit *K-9*. Those whose intellect and physical senses have been all but destroyed by concussive grenades will want to see *Independence Day*, with Will Smith.

Keep watching, my friends, and, above all, enjoy yourselves. Together we will find another *Road House*, and every last one of us will then be bouncers who find love and confront our demons at a small bar just outside of Kansas City. You know, metaphorically speaking.

PART ONE

ANNNND...*ACTION!*

VOLCANO

I hate to start this thing by nitpicking, believe me, but the movie really should have been called *Lava*, not *Volcano*. The film, starring Tommy Lee Jones and Anne Heche, really was long on lava and, as far as I could tell, had only one small—quite small, really—volcano. *And*, despite all the hype, the coast was not, at any time during the film, toast. The coastal *city* of Los Angeles, California, was indeed in no small danger of being incinerated by flowing magma, but the situation was competently handled by disaster workers, and only the most pessimistic naysayer would describe the situation by saying, rather unhelpfully, "The coast is toast."

You may accuse me of being rather picayune, but when a film endlessly hypes—on television, radio, the sides of buses, billboards, drink mugs, cheese-erito wrappers, Fruit Roll-Up packages, the underside of dirigibles, and family-size toilet tissue packs—that "The Coast Is Toast!," I expect to see the entire coast—say, from Long Beach to Oakland—and every one of its millions of inhabitants

incinerated into unrecognizable char. Do not misunder-
stand me. I don't actually have a desire to *see* that; I just
want my expectations managed with more integrity.

In the first act of *Volcano: The Film That Shamefully Mis-
represents Its Content,* we learn that Stan Olber, head of the
Metropolitan Transit Authority, and Mike Roark (Tommy
Lee Jones), head of the Office of Emergency Manage-
ment, have trouble cooperating when their respective
jurisdictions overlap. If that plotline doesn't get your
blood boiling, then perhaps the story of the seismologist
who is reluctant to be interviewed on camera will. I understand they cut the scene in which the City Registrar col-
lated taxpayer information because it was too graphic.

Things pick up when seven transit workers are burned
to death right near the La Brea Tar Pits. Actually anyone
who's been talked into driving more than a mile to see the
La Brea Tar Pits has indeed been burned, badly. There's
not much to see, and parking is hardly convenient. Anyway, seismologist Dr. Amy Barnes (Anne Heche) is
brought in to investigate the incident, and she soon warns
the shar-pei-faced Tommy Lee that the titular volcano may
be forming under their feet. Then the movie pretty much
follows the plot of *Earthquake* (in Sensurround), and you
half-expect to see George Kennedy yelling at Lloyd Nolan,
or Richard Roundtree hanging with Marjoe Gortner.

There's some good special effects as the lava flows
down Wilshire Boulevard, burning up all the Koo Koo
Roo's, Carl's Jr., In and Out Burgers, Jack in the Box, El
Pollo Loco, and all those other chain restaurants with the
incredibly stupid names that L.A. seems to love so much.

And just what does Carl's Jr. mean? Carl's Junior . . . *what?* Carl's burger is junior? Or is it referring to persons younger than Carl? If Carl's restaurant is junior, then there'd need to be a larger restaurant named "Carl's Sr." to put it in the proper context, and *there is no "Carl's Sr."* Again, nitpicking, perhaps, but you just can't go around naming things nonsensically and expecting everyone to buy into it. If I named my store "Clean White Cotton Underpants," and then you came in and discovered I sold nothing but custom kitchen cabinets, you'd be upset, and you'd have every right to be! Or if I called my restaurant "Phil's Double," and then just left it at that, with no explanation, I'd be hurting a lot of people. That's how I feel about "Carl's Jr." I'm hurt and angry.

As for *Volcano,* I was neither hurt nor angered by it. I liked it. Perhaps I was drunk on nitrates from all the luncheon meat I had had that day, or perhaps the botanicals in my wife's hair products that I accidentally used made me susceptible to corny scripts, but I found it pretty entertaining. It was kind of like an old war movie—really cornball, but with a heart. It's not my favorite movie ever (that would be *Heartbeeps*), but it's a decent stupid disaster movie delivery system.

My fear is that its success will lead to more films with clever tag lines, like, say, for a film about a rocket aimed at a town in New York called *Buffalo Shot,* the tag line would be, "Watch Upstate Go Down." Hmmm, that's not very good. Okay, the movie depicts a horrible avalanche in Denver. It's called *Snowball's Chance,* and the line reads, "Colorado, Rocky Mountain DIE." Ew. That's terrible. Try a film about a paramilitary group taking over a Missouri landmark called *Arch Nemeses*. The poster would read, "St. Louie Is Kablooie."

Oh, I like that. I've got to call Casey at Universal and get this baby on the fast track.

THE SHADOW

The kids today, with their Britney Spears, their Ethernets, their Thinsulate® gloves, their oil-filled baseboard heaters . . . they think they got it all over us. Well, maybe I'm old-fashioned, but I remember a time when we didn't have MP3 or other highfalutin compression codes; data was uncompressed—*and we liked it that way!* There was no Marilyn Manson to be seen anywhere—we had Alice Cooper, *and he was perfectly satanic for us, thank you very much!* But people today don't want to remember a time when we took our phaetons out for a hamburger sandwich and some ice cream, a time when the family would gather around the wireless to hear the latest from Wally Phillips or Steve Dahl. Both of them are dead now, of course, but their ghosts still haunt. . . . Hang on, my wife informs me that neither one of them is dead. Steve Dahl still broadcasts out of Chicago, and Wally Phillips only recently retired. She also informs me that we've never had a phaeton. I might suggest that if she were charitable she would allow that our '94 Passat

Wagon, which had four doors and a kind of convertible luggage cover, would *technically* qualify as a phaeton . . . but I don't want to suggest that, not right now, anyway.

Sadly, most people, like my ultramodern wife, have forgotten there ever was a golden age of radio, a time when *Who Needs Klaus* was on right after *The Be Flat Sing-A-Long Brigade.* When I'd sit in my Dr. Denton's, nearly on tenterhooks waiting for *Barnabus Buzzby: Agent From K.I.L.L. . . .*

All right, look—I confess, there never was any gathering around anything to listen to any *Who Needs Klaus*es or *Barnabus Buzzby*s. The truth is I grew up in the '70s and '80s, and I still can't accept the fact that my nostalgia is Jack Wagner and Styx. I want there to have been *Rocket Roswell: Space Patrol* in my past. But all I've got is Gary Numan's "Cars." The synthesizer solo in the middle eight erodes my self-esteem.

That's why I was so excited to see Alec Baldwin in *The Shadow,* the latest film version of the classic pulp drama that I couldn't get enough of as an eager kid, slopping down wheat tailings and saving pennies for a bit of fondant.

The film begins by showing how Ying Ko (Baldwin), an industrious and committed Chinese opium dealer, is kidnapped and then bullied into becoming Lamont Cranston by a do-good holy man. The holy man espouses a kind of vague philosophy ("we are all light and shadow") but never gets down to brass tacks—is he Presbyterian, Missouri-Synod Lutheran? We never learn. Neither do we learn why Alec Baldwin is accepted by other Chinese opium dealers as one of their own, never once inquiring,

"Hey, why are we listening to that guy from Massapequa again?"

Once converted to the holy man's ways, Ying Ko is taught, according to an on-screen slate, "to cloud men's minds—to fog their vision through force of concentration, leaving visible the only thing he can never hide: his shadow." How does that amount to a philosophy of good? What if I just went around clouding men's minds, stealing their Land Rovers and calfskin briefcases, and then claiming, "Well, I was just fogging their minds?"

Besides, as a weapon, fogging men's minds isn't the most potent thing going. As a man, my mind is fogged about 86 percent of the time, anyway. Trying to remember where I stored the glass top that goes with my patio table, *that* fogs my mind; but it doesn't imbue the misplaced tabletop with special powers. (I do like to anthropomorphize any lost item and attribute evil characteristics to it, but I recognize that as *my* weakness—and so does my family.)

Getting back to *The Shadow,* the holy man outplaces his new charge, now named Lamont Cranston (after the mediocre blues band that had a hit with *Upper Mississippi Shakedown*), in New York City, giving him vague instructions to fight crime. He does what he can with this limited "fogging men's minds" power, but mostly he beats up doughy mobsters and laughs that annoying laugh of his. You know, the one that's supposed to be mysterious but just comes off as kind of forced. "Who knows what evil lurks in the hearts of men? Ha ha ha ha ha ha . . ." Yeah, okay. The Shadow knows, though The Shadow seems to be having a lot more fun with it than the rest of us.

He enlists a web of informants by pretending to be magnanimously saving their lives, but then shanghais them into his less-than-profitable organization. He's obviously aware of the limitations of his "fogging men's minds" power and is smart enough to know he needs damn good reconnaissance. He initiates communication with his web by reciting the completely inconspicuous line "The sun is shining," to which the informant must respond, "Yes, but the ice is slippery," a line that works 67 percent of the time in late December through mid-January and then begins to show its strain. A better line might have been, "The humidity is higher than I thought," the response being, "What did you think it was going to be?" Then a higher security check with the line "I thought it would be around seventy percent because of the high pressure system, but the jet stream pushed warmer air from the south up into the cold Canadian front and created this rain and consequently the much higher humidity level." Anyone from Minnesota could hear that exchange and not bat an eye.

The lonely Cranston meets a woman (Penelope Ann Miller) and is immediately intrigued with her because she can read men's thoughts. That's fine for him, but frankly, what woman *can't* read a man's thoughts? Even if she had no innate ability to read men's minds and guessed "I'd really like some ham," she'd be right most of the time. Try "Boy, that Roy Firestone is funny," and the percentages shoot even higher. The only people who can't successfully read men's minds are other men, despite their clumsy attempts at it—most of which involve saying, "You okay, man?"

The Shadow's trouble begin when Shiwan Khan (John Lone), the last survivor of Genghis Khan, comes to New York via a large aluminum sarcophagus in order to explode the atom bomb and take over the world. Please don't ask me who Shiwan Khan is or where he came from. It seems to be a holdover from the comic book version, and those comic book guys get really mad if you question anything. All that I know is Shiwan Khan has the power to hypnotize virtually anyone he wants, and is not limited to merely "fogging men's minds." Cranston finds Shiwan in the Monolith Hotel, which Khan has hidden by hypnotizing every single person in New York City, even the guy who burned my white dress shirt and refused to pay for it.

Shiwan and Cranston do battle, flinging sharp things at each other's skulls by using the method of concentration taught by their mutual friend "the holy man." I have no desire to raise a contentious issue, but aren't holy men, even those of the most obscure and unpopular sects, forbidden from flinging razor-sharp slivers of glass into other men's motor cortexes?

That remains my big stumbling block with *The Shadow*—I don't believe he's good just because the movie asserts that he is. He punches, shoots, and stabs people. I see no community work, no tithing or fasting; the guy's a spiritual mess.

If Ying Do/Lamont Cranston/The Shadow can get his stuff together and figure out what he stands for, I'm ready to sit in front of the warm glow of the Philco with a bowl of treacle and wait for episode two.

THE SAINT

St. John Eudes is remembered for being a brilliant preacher, a wise, compassionate man, and one wholly devoted to his faith. Whether caring for victims of the plague, founding rehabilitation homes for "fallen women," or preaching on the Sacred Heart of Jesus, he was loved by all who were blessed enough to know him.

He must have a lousy agent, though, because he didn't even get a mention, not a *mention*, mind you, in the hot Val Kilmer vehicle *The Saint*. St. Peter Damien, sure. Thomas More, yes. Louis Guanella, of course. Martin de Porres, natch—and all he did was bilocate and fly. St. John Eudes must be feeling pretty lousy right now. He's probably trying to sell a script about his life, can't even get a bite from Miramax or Gramercy, poor dope.

The Saint is based on the works of writer Leslie Charteris, a man with so little self-respect, he allowed himself to be given a woman's name. Has he no sense of shame, running around with a name far less manly than Susan or Debbie or even Linda? You didn't see Hemingway gadding about asking people to call him Betty Hemingway, thank goodness. And you've never read a spy novel by Candy le Carré. So why didn't Charteris have the decency to at least request the nickname "Rocket" or "Chubbs" or even Leslie "Tom" Charteris?

I've never read Tammi's books, so keep in mind any criticism is of the *film,* not of the books, which I'm told are just fine in small doses. In Phillip Noyce's film, Val Kilmer stars as the smooth burglar-for-hire Simon Templar, so named because he was whipped by a Jesuit when he was a boy in the Far East (don't ask me why Jesuit-whipped boys from the Far East are named Simon Templar; I'm just reporting what I saw). Enraged by his caning, he attempts an escape from his school, pausing just long enough to kill his girlfriend and get caught. We then flash-forward to the present, where the grown-up Simon Templar is plotting to steal a microchip from some Super-Evil Russians, completely unaware that microchips are as cheap as salt and readily available from several hundred different on-line sources. (Someone should call that Jessica Charteris and let him know, before the second printing of his *Saint* book comes out.)

As punishment for his microchip theft, the Super-Evil Russians hire Templar to steal the formula for cold fusion (again, don't ask me), which has been developed by the cute and giggly Dr. Emma Russell (Elisabeth Shue). Templar decides to seduce the guileless doctor and so takes on the persona of a greasy, gay German with hair extensions and leather pants. He mumbles, he doesn't tell her his name, his accent is vague. He gets drunk and cuts his head open on their first date. He's like the worst kind of stalker. And yet his plan works perfectly! She can't wait to bed this thick-tongued lubricious Teuton.

Women, really, be truthful—the disturbed poet thing, does it work? I've been on dates where my hair was unkempt; I've slurred my words and said vague, disturbing things; I've even cut myself and shouted Poe up to third-floor windows. Only my bland, unthreatening looks and my ability to whimper have kept me out of jail. Yet Val Kilmer beds Elisabeth Shue without even writing a song with her name in it or punching a parking meter.

Perhaps if my hair were just *that* much longer and greasier, or if my lines had been just a little less concrete. In *The Saint* she asks him who he is, and he actually says, "Just a traveler searching for purity" (actually, "Chust a twaveler zerching for pew-wa-tee," but I translated). I don't know if this line was in that Margaret guy's books, but, *man,* is that bad.

He steals the cold fusion formula from her bra and sells it to the Russians, which only makes her love him more. Again, I've done nothing more than sneeze several months into a really solid relationship, and been dumped like a leftover mackerel. She chases him to Russia, and they are soon both in the clutches of the Super-Evil Russians. They escape, of course, and Templar gets hypothermia. Dr. Russell must then lie nude on top of him to save his life.

Now, I've feigned hypothermia more times than I'd like to admit, once even legitimately dropping my core temperature to eighty-seven degrees Fahrenheit, yet not once did a woman even get near me (excepting the elderly emergency room nurse). Templar, in his first shot at the ancient "hypothermia" gag, gets the beautiful and enchanting inventor of cold fusion to lie starkers spang on top of him! This fellow Rachel's books must really be a hoot.

It all ends when the Super-Evil Russian Guy, who is an enormously popular political figure, states publicly that he doesn't think cold fusion will work. When it does work, they toss him out on his ear, arrest him, and give him life in prison. It's a very fickle constituency. With the Russian out of the way, Templar is free to go on feigning injuries and disorders in order to seduce giggly experts in obscure fields.

It's all pretty stupid, whether or not you can blame that Jane guy who wrote the books. The whole movie seems like an excuse for Val Kilmer to wear stupid wigs and speak in half-baked accents. He's like Jerry Lewis without the dignity.

There's an extra audio track on the DVD edition featuring director Phillip Noyce. He recounts with admiration how when he first met Kilmer, who was working on *The Ghost and the Darkness,* he had a wig-maker living in his tent with him, preparing the wigs for the upcoming shoot. A wig-maker living with him? What is he, Elton John? When I want a nice cut of sirloin, I don't invite the butcher from SuperValu to live with me in order to begin preparing the meat months in advance. But, then, it's well known that Val Kilmer is difficult to work with, a fact that I have to admit needles me. He's Val Kilmer, not Edmund Kean! He's been in *The Island of Dr. Moreau, Willow, Real Genius,* and *Batman Forever*! You don't deserve to be difficult after working with Pat Hingle and Drew Barrymore. Once you've been in a film that featured Kevin Pollack as a squeaky-voiced little fairy, you've forfeited the right to be difficult. Val Kilmer being difficult is like Jaleel White being difficult—he's Urkel, there is no room for difficult.

After seeing *The Saint,* I'm afraid I have to humbly suggest that that guy Karen Charteris go back to the drawing board on the whole idea. And the next time he makes a film version, get someone less difficult.

Brando's available.

SNAKE EYES

If Hollywood action movies are to be believed, our world is constantly being rescued from utter horror, terrorism, and ruin by a small cache of brave, grime-streaked men in ripped T-shirts. They dispense arch wordplay as they vanquish the hateful, vaguely European men who would bring about our destruction. Thankfully Hollywood does not have to be believed, and I am free to reject all they're proposing about Brendan Fraser as well.

But is there something to their theory? Could it be that at virtually every public event I attend there is a well-armed paramilitary group in the boiler room? In each locked stall of the men's room there's a former member of the elite Lithuanian guard just locking a clip into his Russian-made TH-896 laser-sighted automatic? That I narrowly avoided getting my neck snapped by a lithe and menacing man with long blond hair when I almost took a wrong turn into the equipment closet? It seems not only plausible, but probable.

The only problem with the theory is that of shared motivation. I can accept the idea that one man could harbor enough resentment to organize and carry out an extremely complex act of terrorism, but it's unlikely that he could pass that outrage on to dozens of others, no matter how enticing a benefits package he offers. It may be easy for me to launch a personal letter-writing campaign against Boston Market after being severely shorted on my meat loaf portion, but I wouldn't expect others to join in. And I seriously doubt that I could pull together a team of thirty-two well-trained mercs to show up at the Market's corporate headquarters packing rocket launchers and several small nuclear devices.

Certainly in many films the motivation is simply money, yet given the failure rate of robbery or extortion schemes that involve many men, countless helicopters, the kidnapping of prime ministers, planting hundreds of not-inexpensive tracking devices, customizing service vans, and also coming up with contingency plans to handle wisecracking off-duty detectives, it would seem easier simply to take that job at cousin Ed's candy store. Instead, these hapless idiots invariably march willingly into death to further their bosses' wholly unworkable scheme.

Such is the case with *Snake Eyes*, Brian De Palma's film starring Nicolas Cage and Gary Sinise. Its villain, military security specialist Kevin Dunne, played by Sinise, is motivated by his anger over the effectiveness of certain kinds of surface-to-air missiles, so he hatches a plot so complex, its chance of success is somewhere in the 1-in-a-million to 1-in-78^{1400} range. His cohorts are highly loyal, and never call in sick even on the nicest of days.

Sinise's pointlessly elaborate plot culminates at an Atlantic City boxing match when the acting secretary of war is assassinated in front of millions of people. Luckily he was killed right before the beer vendor collected the money for his twenty-two-ounce Budweiser, saving his estate hundreds of dollars. The doors to the arena are locked, and all fourteen thousand people are held as witnesses, forced to eat nothing but the metric-ton piles of cold-boiled shrimp off the casino's buffet until questioned and released. Cage, playing fast-talking Atlantic City cop Rick Santoro, is Dunne's best friend, and is in the front row as his guest when the shooting takes place. Though on duty and actively guarding the secretary of war, Dunne is allowed to invite boozy frat buddies to sit with him while he works. He must have a pretty cool boss who doesn't even care what he does, man. I had that for a while at the Chicken Shack till he freaked on me when he caught me sparking a doob in the walk-in cooler.

While reviewing the Pay-Per-View tape of the event (even as a cop reviewing evidence, he has to pay $59.99 for it), Santoro discovers that the heavily favored champ has taken a fall. (Probably a wise move, considering how doughy he was. He must have had Paul Prudhomme as his trainer.) His investigation points to a mysterious woman with bad vision wearing a blond wig. I would have immediately suspected Carol Channing, but Santoro apprehends a frightened young woman who claims to have seen Dunne plotting the shooting with his loyal and friendly staff. Santoro must then face off against his old friend Dunne, and hope that if he kills him, he still has enough friends to fill out his Friday night broom hockey team.

Dunne eventually reveals his evil plan, in true *Batman*-villian style, and then proceeds to beat the stuffing out of his oldest friend. It made me wonder, if only for a second, whether any of my dear friends are secretly evil supercriminals masterminding the assassinations of key political figures, and are willing at any time to beat me into total submission. You know, I bet my friend Dave is, now that I think of it. That bastard! I know what it is, too—it's that damn credit card bill from T. J. Hooligan's that he says I owe half of. I paid him for that! Only he doesn't remember, the stupid supercriminal that he is! Remind me to call the Secret Service.

Anyway, *Snake Eyes* starts out fine, with a lot of energy and a compelling visual style, but then it quickly loses it, barely ending up ahead of your average Jean-Claude Van Damme film. The visuals overwhelm the characters, which puts a strange distance on the whole experience, as though you're watching it through the front window while standing out on the sidewalk (something I do myself with much less frequency since the Adlerian counseling).

I was so dissatisfied with *Snake Eyes* that I've assembled a crack team of ex-KGB weapons experts and am working on a plan to get my $2.95 rental fee back.

Where's the Super Bowl being played this year?

VAN DAMME

Jean-Claude Van Damme—The Muscles from Brussels. Kick Boxer. Actor. Restaurateur. Dumber than a bag of hammers. Accent thicker than waffle batter. No taller than your average borzoi. Makes Steven Seagal look like Richard Burbage.

Yes, he's all of these things. Yet so much more.

No matter what you think of Mr. Claude Van Damme, you have to agree on one thing: He's not a good actor. Wait, two things: He's not a good actor, and he's really not that good a kick boxer. Hold on, no matter what you think of him, you have to agree on three things: the actor thing, the kick boxer thing, and the fact that he is, in all probability, a thoroughly loathsome human being. All other aspects of him remain a mystery.

The fact that you and I even know who he is stands as testimony to the sad fact that, as we try to understand, even manage, the human struggle entire, some things fall through the cracks, and occasionally, despite our best efforts, chunk-headed muscle guys from Belgium end up as trillionaires, everyone else standing by scratching their heads wondering how it happened. But we mustn't blame ourselves. We mustn't become bitter. We must act with charity toward the sawed-off little lummox.

Through all of Mr. Claude Van Damme's films, from *Bloodsport* to *Cyborg,* from *Universal Soldier* to *Death Warrant,* one theme remains constant: a pitiable chunk of Walloon butt-steak knocking the stuffing out of someone even dumber than himself. Few filmmakers have been as true to their vision as Mr. Claude Van Damme. One other theme remains constant: me watching his films and then complaining, and then watching the next one, till I've seen pretty much everything he's done.

Including two of his most recent films, *Timecop* and *Sudden Death,* both directed by the profoundly not-very-good Peter Hyams.

It's obvious that *Sudden Death* sprang from a simple idea: "Let's make a *Die Hard* rip-off, only instead of it being a so-so movie, let's make it really stupid and hard to watch, with laughable, cookie-cutter characters and a plot that has open contempt for its audience. Oh, and let's make it morally reprehensible, with children being repeatedly terrorized and subjected to horrors beyond imagining!" Sure, a simple idea in theory. But, as we all know, much harder to execute. And this, *Sudden Death* does with aplomb.

The plot involves an evil superhypervillain, played by Powers Boothe, committing acts of terrorism at the final game of the Stanley Cup. If you ask me, the filmmakers are fighting an uphill battle to get their audience to actually *care* if acts of terrorism are committed at *any* hockey game, but I'm only a casual fan, so what do I know? Jean-

Claude Van Damme You All To Hell plays a fire inspector who thwarts his plan every step of the way. This despite the fact that he's very, very stupid.

It all ends with Powers Boothe being gruesomely murdered by our protaganist. So, I suppose some good came of it. Still, I have a beef and here it is.

They had to reshoot scenes from *A Fish Called Wanda* because focus groups were absolutely horrified by scenes of a dog being accidentally killed. Yet in *Sudden Death* no less than a dozen human beings are callously, brutally murdered, many of them in front of an eight-year-old girl, our hero's daughter. Most of the murders are used as punch lines to Powers Boothe's jokes.

All this because some Antwerp knucklehead got teased in high school.

That aside, *Timecop* is a much better film. In it, Damme attempts to answer questions only superficially understood by Einstein, Bohr, and Hawking. His conclusion: Time travel is best used to go back a few years and kick the stuffing out of supervillain Ron Silver.

Yes, Jean Damme is . . . a Timecop. One of those hardworking, yet in my opinion shamefully underpaid, civil servants who polices the comings and goings of rogue time travelers. Ron Silver plays an evil senator who approved money for the Timecop division and is now using the technology to steal money from the past for his current presidential run. There's boundless vision for you. You can travel anywhere in the history of Earth itself—the Mesozoic, Mycenae 1600 B.C., the time of Christ? Thank you, no. I'm fine with petty Civil War robberies in an attempt to prop up my sagging presidential bid.

In the end, Silver's character finds out that matter can't occupy the same space at the same time. Or, as Claude Damme might say, "Mahter canoot hockupie da seem spice ot da seem tahm."

If you must rent a Jean Damme movie (and, as an American, you must) rent *Timecop*. As Jean Van might say, "Theyra air much wahrs wais fowr ewe to spaynd on ivineeng."

Ask every man, woman, and child in this nation what the greatest country in the world is and I'll bet you my last dollar that 27.35 percent of 'em will sing right back, "Why, the United States of America!! Who's askin'? And, hey, when do I get my check?" Another 36 percent are likely to say Japan, Canada, or France, while a good 8 percent will say, "The Fatherland," and a frustrating .7 percent will say, "Utah."

Yes, this is largely a great country, and despite Idaho and chunks of California, we can be sure that we're one of the five best countries in the Northern Hemisphere.

We're beginning to hit our stride in several important areas, and we can say with genuine pride that we do a couple of things really well: We throw a good parade; we offer a number of quality off-the-rack suit jackets; and we drop-forge a fairly decent spoon. Oh, and we make some good action movies.

These are unassailable truths, as dear to us as whipped goose organs are to your average Frenchman.

Yet an unassuming Chinese man threatens one of these

basic tenets. Yes, let Hollywood be warned. Jackie Chan has come to kick ass and make tiger prawn dumplings, and he's all out of bamboo steamers and ginger dipping sauce!

Chan is the real thing, and frankly, he makes Van Damme look like a brick-stupid, hairless Belgian ape. He makes Stallone look like a five-foot-four pile of lukewarm carpaccio. He makes Schwarzenegger look like a no tal-ent, Humvee-driving Aryan.

Chan has been a hit in mainland China and in Japan for many years but has made almost no impression in the United States, until now. This is probably because his films were unable to gain a foothold in a crowded field that included *Mannequin, North Dallas Forty,* and *Prancer.* It's also quite possible that American studio executives felt certain we wouldn't understand Chan's unique blend of martial arts, comedy, and action. So they made *Teen Wolf* instead.

Chan has made several half-baked attempts to conquer the American market before. Once in the Scotch-fueled Hal Needham effort, *The Cannonball Run I* and *II,* and once in the Danny Aiello yawner *The Protector.* I was thrilled that two of his most recent efforts, *Rumble in the Bronx* and *Supercop,* were widely released, saving me the effort of pawing through stacks of videos at Asian markets, where large, clumsy Midwesterners with a propensity to tip over stacks of dried black fungus are not a welcome sight.

Rumble in the Bronx, though a fairly stupid movie, does offer some vintage Chan in the way of stunts and special effects. In it, Chan plays a Chinese man who comes to

America to help his uncle with his store in the Bronx. Much like Kane in *Kung Fu,* he immediately runs afoul of the local toughs, who, to my eye, look no tougher than the seventh-season cast of *Fame.* Perhaps that's enough, when one takes into consideration Jesse Borrego, Nia Peeples, and that one keyboard player who looks like a cross between Lou Ferrigno and Billy Squier.

Chan squares off with the ersatz members of the High School for the Performing Arts and ends up befriending the disabled nephew of one of their members. Then, as often happens in the Bronx, a merciless drug syndicate (as opposed to the less prevalent "caring and lenient" drug syndicate) uses the wheelchair of Chan's young friend to hide a stash of diamonds.

Chan mends his fences with the *Flashdance*-ian gang of rakehells and chides them, "You are all scum."

"He's right," they agree, and soon are working together against the drug lords.

I can't say it's not a dumb movie, yet as an introduction to Jackie Chan, you could do a lot worse. Much of it quite obviously wasn't filmed in the Bronx, and the dubbing is only marginally better than your average kung fu film, yet as entertainment, it's worth six *Last Action Hero*s, two dozen *The Specialist*s, and several hundred Van Damme films, your choice.

Supercop is a much better film. It was in wide release only recently, though it was made several years earlier. I saw it in small release under the title *Supercop II,* if memory serves. It was a subtitled release, and I was forced to see it at one of those stinky art houses where one normally must sit next to hairy-legged men and women with questionable hygiene who overcompensate by bathing in patchouli oil. Not content to simply watch films, they are compelled to trade Peter Greenaway arcana sotto voce and mumble things like "so true" whenever clumsy scenes of oppression appear onscreen.

Still, even they could not dim my enthusiasm for *Super-cop*. The stunts that Chan pulls off are simply incredible, and certainly quite illegal if filmed in the United States. I won't even go into plot, for it barely matters. Just see it.

In fact, if you must see a Schwarzenneger film, pay for a Chan film and sneak in to see Arnie.

BROKEN ARROW/ EXECUTIVE DECISION

If action movies had any basis in reality, wise-cracking terrorists would be holding the country hostage every forty-eight hours, and Earth's future would be in the hands of thick-tongued lunkheads like Jean-Claude Van Damme. Personally, I'm uncomfortable with that. I wouldn't let Jean-Claude Van Damme feed my fish, let alone negotiate mercurially complicated hostage crises. I'd prefer that Jimmy Carter be involved and Jean-Claude be left behind and told that the terrorists ordered him to peel several tons of new potatoes. World peace is too important a job to be left to someone who pronounces it "warald piss."

These complaints aside, I like the action movie. Though most people complain they don't have enough hours in the day, I'm left with too many and nothing to do once I've solved the puzzle on the back of the Fruit Brute cereal box. Nothing kills the hours faster than a good action movie.

I've just seen two with a jaunty aeronautical theme that I can recommend wholeheartedly: the Travolta/Slater/

Mathis (Samantha, not Johnny) opus, *Broken Arrow*, and the Steven Seagal/Kurt Russell attempt, *Executive Decision*.

Broken Arrow is the somewhat implausible tale of a pilot, played by Travolta, who hijacks several nuclear weapons in an attempt to hold the world hostage simply because he's been passed over for promotion several times. Why can't he just key his boss's Lexus or clog up the toilet in the executive washroom? Well, because he's crazy. And so he creates a plan so Rube Goldbergian, involving dozens of not-so-bright men doing hundreds of intricately timed, labor-intensive tasks, that it has a one in eighty-nine bajillion chance of succeeding. Left to his own devices, Travolta most surely would have crashed the first of thousands of planes, helicopters, Humvees, trains, and elevators that are part of his plot into the first tree he saw and been sitting at the side of the road crying when they found him. Instead, his ex-partner, played by Christian Slater, and a park ranger, Samantha Mathis, encourage the poor dope by attempting to foil his snowball's-chance-in-hell scheme.

It all gives Travolta a chance to overact with a zeal that makes Ron Palillo's Horshack look impossibly dignified and bottomlessly reserved. No scenery is safe from his hungry jaws. Even the rock-headed gridiron palooka Howie Long, as one of Travolta's team, looks like John Houseman next to the histrionics of the gesticulating sweathog.

The Utah depicted in the film is a place replete with nuclear devices, weapons storehouses, and million-pound freight-loads of vague and apocalyptically explosive liquids. This may be true, for all I know. Someone should check on it. Now that I think of it, is anyone keeping an eye on Utah? What goes on out there? Well, Van Damme can check on it later.

Executive Decision is my favorite movie ever, if only because it killed off Steven Seagal very early into the film. The greasy, thick-skulled mumbler is exactly the kind of person we need less of in this world. He reminds me of my old gym coach, a chilling association. All gym coaches everywhere are evil, if you'll allow me this tiny prejudicial statement, and none should be allowed to walk the streets freely, let alone exact their horrible revenge for shortcomings unthinkable on impressionable and mentally stable youth. Each and every one should be caned with wet rattan, pelted with red rubber playground balls, and sent to Devil's Island.

Thank you.

As for the movie, sans Seagal, it actually manages to maintain short bursts of tension and is refreshingly free of the humorless, staccato clichés that teem around every other flick in the genre. Plus, I can't help it, I like Kurt Russell. He and Goldie Hawn have most assuredly made some unholy pact with the fallen angel, that they manage to look a lithesome twenty-nine when they are in fact both over eighty, and without the pained, sandblasted look of the horrible Frankenstein's monster that Cher has become. But forgiving him that, he's a likable chap, and I wouldn't mind getting a beer with him, my highest praise.

The plot of *E.D.*, as its fans call it, involves some Middle Eastern terrorists skyjacking a 747 loaded with a poison nerve gas that they intend to rain down on Washington, D.C. There's no downside, as far as I can see, but the residents of our nation's capital feel differently and so enlist Seagal, a special forces man, and Russell, an expert on terrorists, to board the plane while airborne and defuse the situation lest the world be deprived of a Newt Gingrich, an Orrin Hatch, or a Dick Armey.

It's not bad, and remember, it's 97 percent Steven Seagal–free! It's 100 percent Jean-Claude Van Damme–free! Enjoy in good health.

I don't get comic books, I admit, so perhaps I'm not qualified to comment on movies based on comic books. Come to think of it, I don't really get movies, either. Neither do I get movie rental store clerks who refuse to look at me even while shouting their demand for my phone number. Still, I rented *Blade* with the hope that it would give me some insight into the inky world of comics. Now I'm even more confounded, saddened, and slightly dyspeptic.

I'd never really seen a comic book close up until a roommate of mine showed me one of those expensive, thicker *Batman* comics from the '80s. It made very little impression on me other than the fact that it was thicker than most comic books and I remember it was more expensive. I have some slight impression that it also made me a little angry, but that might be misplaced anger at my roommate, a man who has showered *maybe* three times since his birth in 1961.

A couple of years after *Batman*, someone sent me copies of a comic book about a slacker and his girlfriend;

the characters were drawn all droopy and dark, they cussed a lot. The title was just one word and it was a verb, I think. *Drip,* or *Fall. Hate,* maybe. I don't remember, I only remember thinking that whatever it was, it wasn't meant for me.

Blade is, as far as I know, based on the comic book *Blade.* I don't know if the comic book starred Wesley Snipes, though I would doubt it.

Snipes plays a self-loathing half-vampire who, in the opening scene, enters a vampire discotheque and opens fire on the children of the night, luckily right before Dead or Alive's "You Spin Me Round" had a chance to queue up. He kills all of them save one, who is brought to the hospital, where it is hoped he can find a doctor who specializes in shape-shifters. He bites his care provider, Dr. Karen Jenson (N'Bushe Wright), who testily suggests he be dropped from his managed care group. Snipes takes her back to his lair for treatment of her lycanthropy and to see if she can't do something with the unruly hair of his right-hand man, Abraham Whistler (Kris Kristofferson). Whistler is a crack vampire-killer weapons manufacturer who also provides Blade with a serum that keeps him from becoming a full-blooded vampire. When he has the sniffles, Whistler also knows which cough medicine is right for Blade.

Once Dr. Karen Jenson has recovered enough to be able to look at Kris Kristofferson without laughing, Blade explains that there is a subculture of vampires living among the humans, and that the Count from *Sesame Street* is just the tip of the iceberg. Whistler tells her the story of how Blade came to be: It turns out Blade is called Blade because he carries several swords, all of them with blades. For a short time he carried sharp sticks and was known as Stick, but there was confusion because that's also the name of a 1985 Burt Reynolds film. When he switched to the plural "Sticks," he found himself at a disadvantage in vampire showdowns because they kept peppering him with questions about "Mr. Roboto" and "Lorelei." Most disastrously, for a whole summer Whistler had him try out a blunderbuss.

Karen follows Blade as he travels the streets at night battling vampires and turning them into 1s and 0s so that they can be rendered as unconvincing effects. His duty done, he goes to Denny's and orders their Grand Slam breakfast, where he substitutes blood for the two eggs, blood for the two pancakes, blood for the two strips of crisp bacon, but keeps the hash browns and just has them with ketchup.

One of his foes, Deacon Frost (Stephen Dorff), has plans to turn all of humanity into vampires by fulfilling an ancient prophecy written of in the vampire bible. Frost is angry because only the dingiest hotels will allow him to place vampire bibles in a drawer of the bedside tables. Even after draining Tom Bodett of his precious fluids, he could only get him to agree to let him put them in the Motel 6 in Prescott, Wisconsin, and San Luis Obispo, California.

Frost uses Blade's blood to summon an ancient vampire god, Ted the Vampire God, who turns out to be something of a wuss, even as ancient vampire gods go. Blade destroys the whole plan, meaning that the only vampire prophecy yet fulfilled is that they be the subjects of stupid movies starring Stephen Dorff.

Unless you're actually scooped up and put into a hopper of discarded animal innards, *Blade* is probably the bloodiest and most gruesome thing you'll ever see in your life. Children under thirty-eight should not be allowed to watch this film, and those over thirty-eight should be hardened by life, their souls tough little chunks of some blackish material. However, as dark as it is, it should be admitted that there are quite a few outstanding dance numbers.

I watched *Blade* on the DVD special edition, which contained more information on the making of *Blade* than there actually *is* information on the making of *Blade*. I thought the four-hour documentary on the catering crew was particularly unnecessary. Come to think of it, *Blade* is probably more *Blade* than anyone will ever need.

ACTION JACKSON/ STONE COLD

The appeal of football has thus far managed to elude me—though I suppose if I were from Texas and drank heavily, I might feel otherwise. But I kid the fans. I just have an aversion to corpulent guys smacking each other's tiny, shimmering buttocks.

So although I can't appreciate the antics of these titans of the gridiron doing battle on the frozen tundra of Lambeau Field, I certainly can appreciate their accomplishments on the silver screen. Though no linebacker-cum-thespian that I can think of has threatened the legacy of Edmund Kean, John Barrymore, or even that one Baldwin brother with the scrunched-up face who is in those Pauly Shore movies, they've made many an entertaining film.

Action Jackson (1988) is just such a movie. Pigskin magician Carl Weathers stars as Jericho "Action" Jackson, a streetwise cop on the edge, etc., etc. Frankly, he's pretty lucky his name is Jackson, and he is so action-oriented as to warrant the nickname "Action," because if his last name were Paulson or Reese or Thibedeau, the title would have lacked the special magic that gives it its appeal. "Carl Weathers *Is* Action Paulson" or "Carl Weathers *Is* Action Thibedeau" would not have worked.

Craig T. Nelson is Action's Moriarty, Peter Dellaplane. You can tell he's evil because he's rich and has a whole can of gray dye in his hair. Sharon Stone plays a woman who wears a backless dress—I think she's Dellaplane's wife or something. She's really blond and tan and appears to be addicted to Dr Pepper lip gloss. Vanity plays Nelson's mistress, a nightclub singer who vacuums up his endless supply of heroin. And speaking of nicknames, is "Vanity" really a good choice? Why not "Bidet," or "Shower Curtain," or some other bathroom fixture?

As delightful a bad movie as it is, I must report a glaring flaw. Early in the film, Dellaplane, in attempting to remember Jackson's nickname, says, "Oh, that's right—it rhymes." Well, no, it doesn't, Mr. Dellaplane. If it rhymed, it would be "Action Jacktion," or "Ackson Jackson," which clearly it is not. If the filmmakers had just dug a little deeper, cared a little more, the line would have read, "Oh, that's right—it utilizes assonance." It's sad to see a movie like this ruined by such a glaring mistake.

Another Sunday warrior, Brian Bosworth, made a much better film—1991's *Stone Cold*. The Bos (or Boz, or Bahz, I'm not really sure) stars as Joe Huff, a streetwise cop on the edge, etc., etc. He's shanghaied by the FBI to infiltrate a gang of bikers led by the evil Chains (Lance Henriksen). In order to fool the wily "brotherhood," Huff "becomes" a biker—he rides a "hog," he refers to his intimate female companion as his "old lady," he throws back some "suds." When prompted, he lifts his T-shirt to reveal his bare breast.

Once in the gang, he takes the name John Stone as a pseudonym. Now, I hate to perseverate on this point, but again, he's lucky the name lent itself to the title's particularly mischievous brand of wordplay, for had it been John Padwerski, John Clementine, or John Cromwell, I can't imagine an exec green-lighting this film. "Brian Bosworth in Padwerski Cold" would not work.

William Forsyth plays Ice, Chains's assistant. Apparently, when he's not directing charming, quirky films like *Gregory's Girl, Comfort and Joy,* and *Local Hero,* he's playing greasy bikers in B movies. Maybe it's a different guy. Anyway, Ice mistrusts Stone (we know he's Joe Huff, but Ice doesn't, the poor dope) and suspects he might be FBI, a cop, or a washed-up football player. Chains likes him instantly because he drinks a lot of Dixie brand beer and can beat guys up. Soon he is on the inside, learning all about the gang's plan to kill the hard-line D.A. and Presbyterian ministers. It's never explained why they're killing Presbyterian ministers. Is it well known that bikers hate Presbyterian ministers, and I just missed it?

It all leads to a showdown at the courthouse, where the scruffy, drunken bikers manage to kill more soldiers than were officially killed in both The Great War *and* WWII.

It's worth sticking around for the credits, where we find out the bikers' names were Gut, Tool, Trouble, Mudfish, A.W.O.L., and Vitamin. To me, it would be a shame to go to all the trouble of being a biker—all the hazing, having to down all that warm, skunky beer, getting prickly heat and odd rashes from infrequently laundered leather pants—only to be given the nickname "Vitamin." Now that I think of it, "Mudfish" isn't going to strike terror in any but the most timorous soul.

I have to go now. I'm working on a screenplay for William "The Refrigerator" Perry. He's a time-traveling cop on the edge named Jake Stitch. The working title is *A Stitch in Time.* Direct all inquiries to my agent.

TWISTER/ INDEPENDENCE DAY

There's a force sweeping through this great nation of ours; you can see it in the heroin-dilated eyes of our youth as they raise Cosmopolitans to their Vandyke-fringed mouths in wan and shallow tribute to our cocktail forefathers; you can smell it in the rich, hand-rubbed leather interiors of the sport-utility vehicles that conquer Blockbuster Videos and Boston Markets alike; and, yes, you can taste it in our Frappaccinos. It's called excess. And it's available now at all participating Subway stores.

Lately, the movie industry has been supersizing things for us with Big Gulp–style films. Big, bad movies with lots of stuff in 'em. As bad as most movies, only bigger. Huge, out-of-control budgets, big as the GNP of Chile or Scandinavia. Enough money to afford flying cows and huge, dumb Bill Paxtons. *Order up a gross more alien ships and buy me a Will Smith!* They're Must-See movies. Not to see them is to risk revocation of citizenship and eventual deportation.

I recently ate a 'Frisco Meal Deal that included *Twister*

and *Independence Day,* two of the biggest dumb-ass movies we as a nation have ever produced.

Twister is the story of an actor named Bill Paxton and how he's not very good. Supporting this story are Jami Gertz, Helen Hunt, Cary Elwes, and the guy who played Cameron in *Ferris Bueller's Day Off.*

It all takes place in a county that must be blighted by God because it experiences 3,700 tornadoes in a four-hour period. Some of them . . . are F5s!!! I learned from *Twister* that F5s are really bad twisters. *Really* bad twisters. If so, *Twister* is an F5 twister. Ha ha ha ha ha ha.

Twister cost, as I understand it, 570 bajillion dollars. Well, I can report it's all up there on the screen. From that one tornado, to that other tornado, to that one other tornado, every penny is up there. The performance of Cary Elwes alone must have cost $35 billion dollars. The only thing they scrimped on was the script, but luckily that's only a tiny part of the *Twister* experience. Some sample dialogue from Michael Crichton's script:

"Come on, run. Get down. Come on, get in. Run. Come on. We might have a chance. Hold on. Come on. Hang on."

Much of *Twister*'s footage was done in the digital domain, with 1s representing incompetence and 0s representing crap.

Overall, I feel that *Twister* delivered on its promise that it was a movie that had tornadoes in it.

In sharp contrast to *Twister, Independence Day* was a bloated, star-gorged production with a lousy script that relied on special effects and sinful advertising budgets. So not really "in sharp contrast" at all. When I said that, I was angry. I was lashing out and I'm sorry.

Independence Day, or *ID4,* as it was called by its marketing department, is the story of aliens invading Earth. It differs from the hundreds of movies from the '50s, '60s, and '70s that featured aliens invading Earth in that it was made in the '90s. To be sure, things exploded in *Independence Day,* as they have in many other, better movies that came before it, but *Independence Day* has the distinction of being *a more recent film* than those made before and therefore *was recently available to be seen at a theater,* a distinct advantage over older, better alien-invasion films that were not recently available to be seen at a theater.

In *Independence Day,* the dependably unappealing Bill Pullman, fresh from his towering performance in *Casper the Friendly Ghost* (based on a Carson McCullers short story), stars as the president of the United States of America, a man clearly unhappy with the fact that his polls are down and that intelligent calamari are wiping out hundreds of thousands of his disloyal constituents. He does the only sensible thing: He enlists the help of a drunk, unshaven Randy Quaid to take on the seemingly omnipotent beings. Mary McDonnell (who should have known better) stars as the first lady, a strong woman unsullied by dirty land deals and bad children's books.

Jeff Goldblum stars as Jeff Goldblum. This time, he's a quirky scientist who knows the true secret of the aliens. The secret he harbors? The aliens plan to invade Earth! He unfortunately learns this only after the aliens have already invaded Earth, so not even his offensive, stereotypical father, played by Judd Hirsch, can convince anyone to listen to his ramblings.

None of this dissuades fighter pilot Will Smith from his brilliant plan of having a girlfriend with large breasts. This he carries out unswervingly.

I can't tell you the end, but I will say that it involves aliens failing to invade Earth.

I don't want you to get the impression that I'm down on the current Hollywood films, because when it gets down to a choice between a big-budget blockbuster and a Krzysztof Kieslowski snore-fest, for me, the coast is toast every time!

I say get yourself a McRib Meal Deal, supersize it, and then, chomp!

FACE/OFF

What if you could have your face cut off, preserved in a strong brine, and then have somebody else's freshly peeled face sewn onto your skull? This is the intriguing premise of *Face/Off,* director John Woo's action blockbuster starring Nicolas Cage and John Travolta.

Personally, if I were going to have my face removed and another's sewn in its place, I'd have them replace my skull while they were at it and give me Allan Fawcett's teeth. As for whose face I'd want sewn in place of mine—Boris Becker's. Then I'd get better tables at restaurants in Europe, and there'd be a buzz about me here in the States, without setting off too much pandemonium to the point where I'd lose my privacy. I'd probably be tempted to try Salma Hayek's face for a while, just to see what it's like. But I realize seeing her smoky beauty riding atop my hideous tower of flesh would challenge, even horrify, your average person. Plus, she'd then be stuck with a huge, whiskery face, and that's bound to hamper her career as a beautiful actress.

The first challenge one confronts with *Face/Off* is the

curious, I might even say *misplaced,* "forward slash" in its title. Are "Face" and "Off" separate talents that the title has on its résumé? Is there a choice between "face" and "off" that we, or one of the movie's characters, are asked to make? Perhaps "Off" is a computer file extension of the program "Face." The slash is even more confounding given the dizzying array of character and punctuation marks one has to choose from. Was *Face%Off* considered and rejected and, if so, why? How did the slash win out over the altogether more approachable * character, or even the ^? I find it most likely that the slash was a later accretion by an ambitious promotions person trying to make a name for herself. "I'm the one who put the slash in *Face/Off*!" one can almost hear her bragging, completely oblivious to the soupy haze of confusion she created.

The film opens with a prologue in which Sean Archer (Travolta) frolics with his son on a merry-go-round while Castor Troy (Cage) spies them both through the scope of his high-powered rifle. It's all done in slow motion, shot with a hazy filter—it looks like a Dean Witter commercial, only with a sniper. Troy shoots and kills Archer's son because, as we'll soon learn, he's really evil.

It's ten years later, and we find out that although Archer is the director of a super-duper-secret-hyper-covert antiterrorism task force, he mostly uses his position to set-tle his personal grudge against Castor Troy. (By the way, *Castor* Troy? He's named after a smelly laxative?) Troy has just planted a bomb at the L.A. Convention Center, a bomb almost as big as the Thirteenth Annual Plastic Lunch Tray Manufacturers Convention that was there the week before. Archer and his agents catch and ostensibly kill Troy as he tries to make his way out of the country. (But not before Troy kills roughly 675 anonymous agents—each death lovingly, almost beautifully filmed in that pornographically violent style we've come to expect from director John Woo.)

Castor's brother Pollux, also captured in the raid, refuses to give any information on where the bomb was planted, and is also closemouthed about where he got his stupid name. This leaves them with little choice but to vacuum the face off of Castor's skull and graft it onto Archer's. You see, Castor is in a coma, being kept alive so that experts can study the effects of pointlessly moronic names. Archer is to masquerade as Castor, enter the prison where Pollux is being held, and fool him into giving up the location of the bomb—tricky work, even when one's head isn't really sore. Archer agrees, mostly because he's excited that he gets to eat all the ice cream he wants for a week after the operation.

Luckily for Archer, the face-transplanting crew has only done three that day, and is still fresh for his. The doctor free-hands a cut around his face, and then a special attachment for the Oreck is placed over his visage, sucking it clean off. It is then placed in an old Mason jar for safekeeping. His hairline is adjusted, stomach is liposuctioned, butt cheeks lifted slightly, and in a couple of days he'll look just like Castor (or Morey Amsterdam, depending on how the scars heal). His voice will be altered by a tiny microchip (developed by Rich Little MicroSystems) implanted in his throat. When Archer finishes his assignment, his useless Castor flesh will be vacuumed off, and his own pickled face will be reattached. It's a perfect plan.

The only possible cock-up would be if the faceless Castor awoke from his coma, kidnapped a microsurgeon, had Archer's preserved face sewn on to his skull, took Archer's position on the terrorist squad, killed anyone who had knowledge of Archer's secret mission, lived with Archer's wife, and taunted the real Archer, who was rotting away in prison with no chance of parole—but the odds of that happening are very slim indeed.

The impossible happens! Now Castor-faced Archer's only chance is to escape from the secret high-security magnetic prison where he's being held. Let me explain: Each prisoner is custom-fitted with electronically controlled boots that can be locked to the steel grid of the prison floor remotely. (The boots, I'd imagine, would price out at about $7,300 a pair; $500 more for the fitting. The monitoring system has to go for at least $23.5 million, not counting upkeep. The structure—an old offshore oil rig in fair condition—$56 million. Staffing, maintenance, software . . . there were about two hundred prisoners being kept there . . . hey! That's over a million dollars per prisoner per year! Of the taxpayer's money!) Castor-faced Archer escapes when they take his boots off to give him electroshock therapy. (Oh. I guess we're paying for that, too!) He enlists the help of Castor's old gang to get back at Archer-faced Castor.

Everyone dies. Except Castor-faced Archer and Archer-faced Castor, that is. They have a battle on two huge power-boats. And then Castor dies. And they peel off Archer's stolen face and plaster it back on his mug like a Post-it note. They don't say whether they reattach Castor's face so he can have an open-casket funeral, but it seems like it would be a nice gesture, even though he was pretty evil.

Face/Off is the dumbest movie you will ever see in your lifetime. It's probably the dumbest movie the whole of human industry could create, even if we started now and were given unlimited time and resources. Travolta and Cage give the biggest, dumbest performances you'll ever see, even if you regularly attend shows featuring huge, animatronic bears singing Carpenters songs.

If it weren't violent and offensive enough to knock a buzzard off a gut-wagon, it would be the most laughable film ever.

Sadly, for John Woo and everyone involved, that honor still belongs to *Road House*.

PART TWO

WILD THANGS

Every now and again, a movie comes along that touches your soul, looses the moorings that hold in place your core beliefs, and makes you look at love in a different light. But they usually take up four laserdisc sides and star Kate Winslet or Sir Ian McKellen. Personally, I don't have the time. Not only for the movie, but for self-inspection and improvement of the spirit. I've got ape movies to look at.

There are many to choose from, and unless you yourself have direct simian ancestry (i.e., if there are apes in your lineage as recent as the eighteenth century), not one will touch your soul or challenge you in any way. Wait, maybe *Dunston Checks In* will, but beyond that, the field is intellectually barren.

Though it's certainly a point for discussion, many will cite *King Kong* as being the first of the great ape movies. Personally, I think one need fast-forward to 1981 and Tony Danza's *Going Ape!* In this comedy, the affable Italian-American cavorts with a trio of orangutans, and seems perfectly at home. (Not to imply that Mr. Danza belongs with other monkeys . . . what I mean is . . . look, never mind!)

So popular is the movie, still, that one is hard-pressed to find it anywhere on video shelves. It is rented far more frequently than the Donny and Marie talkie, *Goin' Cocoanuts,* a film it often shares shelf space with.

Some will take issue, perhaps even hurt me, for skipping right over *Every Which Way but Loose,* Clint Eastwood's 1978 orangutan buddy flick (written by Jeremy Joe Kronsberg, who directed *Going Ape!*). I say, an important step in the ape movies' evolution, yes, but you already had the tough and cantankerous Ruth Gordon, so to me, the orangutan was something of a redundancy, comedically speaking. (I don't mean to imply that Ms. Gordon was apelike, I just . . . well, why don't I just stop right here).

My point is that *E.W.W.B.L.,* as its fans call it, had a plotline that had little to do with the monkey itself, and everything to do with Clint knocking the stuffing out of other long-neck-quaffing losers. (Not to imply that Mr. Eastwood is a long-neck-quaffing loser . . .)

Anyway, it is but sound and fury, mere monkey Entre'act to last year's *Ed,* the hit comedy starring *Friends*'s Matt LeBlanc, or Matt The White in his native country.

In *Ed,* Mr. The White is a losing pitcher on a losing quadruple-A ball club who is put in charge of the team's mascot, Ed, a *chimpanzee*! Ed is kind of the Wild Thing of this movie, Wild Thing being the character played by prostitute industry bankroller Charlie Sheen in *Major League.* Ed plays baseball, saves the team, contracts Lou Gehrig's disease, and announces to the crowd that "today . . . I feel . . . like the luckiest . . . ape . . . in the world." Okay, I made the last part up. Along the way to victory, however, Ed and The White have to contend with an amoral, monomaniacal baseball owner, sort of the Ted Turner of this movie. (Not to imply that Ted Turner is amoral and monomaniacal. Except that he is.)

The hardest thing to take about this movie is Ed himself. He's not a real chimpanzee but a man inside a suit with a frightening servo-controlled mask on. The monkey simulacrum is close enough, but not so close that it tricks you, so it ends up being downright disturbing. If you were making *Exorcist II: Any Which Way You Can,* it would be perfect.

The humor relies heavily on foul scatology, and though no one is a bigger fan of foul scatology than I, after the thirty-five hundredth example of chimpanzee flatulence, I grew weary. To say something nice, it really isn't any worse than *The Canterbury Tales.*

As for the puppy-dog-eyed LeBlanc, well, maybe he got bad advice from his agent. Or perhaps someone blew a handful of that mind-control drug used by South American cartels into his face and told him to do this movie. Then showed up on set every day and blew more mind-controlling drugs into his face on an hourly basis. The scene where LeBlanc wants to use his bathroom and Ed's in there will live forever, a constant reminder than man has so far to go; that dignity is not granted but must be achieved; that as we strive for grace and wisdom, we fall, broken, and find ourselves pounding on the door to the crapper where an ape poops all over our magazines.

I wonder if his *Friends* friends were "there for him." I saw a sad photo of the perky Jennifer Aniston slinking out of the premiere of *Ed,* a pained smile on her face. But, hey! She was in that Ed Burns stink-burger, *She's the One.* What's she all high and mighty for? And David Schwimmer, he starred in *The Pallbearer,* and that was no trip to Hollywood, either! And Courteney Cox was in *Ace Ventura, Pet Detective,* for crying out loud!

I say go, Matt. Make *Ed II* and stand tall, if you can.

THE GHOST AND THE DARKNESS

"What is it that frightens you most?" This question has fascinated filmmakers and authors for many years. Stephen King has written a book a day on the subject for the last twenty-five years. His latest novel, *The Devil's Tweezers,* plays on people's fear of splinters. It's the story of a large splinter that killed a logger in 1876 and is dug up by a suburban housewife. The splinter uses the soul of the logger to dig itself deep into the palm of those who cross it. Tomorrow he's writing a book about people's fear of speaking in front of a group. It's called *Toastmaster Devil.*

My greatest fear is that of being buried alive in Roquefort cheese, followed closely by a suffocating fear that I'll be stuck in an elevator with my UPS guy, a jittery man with hollow, hunted eyes, who stands four inches closer than personal comfort allows. Many people have a fear of flying, but that can usually be attributed to post-traumatic stress brought about by those large businessmen who spread their legs wide apart, not at all troubled by the amount of leg-to-leg contact they share with their row-mates. Others fear aging, and many, many people find no relief from their fear of Ed O'Neill.

Stephen Hopkins's film *The Ghost and the Darkness* plays off our fear of being eaten by lions. Being eaten by lions while working on a bridge over the Tsavo River in 1898, that is. I think we've all felt that fear at one time or another. Whether or not you fear the less-than-dignified performance by Michael Douglas is another matter.

The Ghost and the Darkness is the chilling sequel to *The Ghost and Mr. Chicken,* in which Don Knotts and Dick Sargent must conspire to solve the mystery behind the "haunted" Simmons mansion. In *The Ghost and the Darkness* Val Kilmer takes the Don Knotts role, only instead of being the town 'fraidy-cat, he's an Irish engineer hired by a hard-nosed industrialist to oversee construction of a bridge in East Africa. Michael Douglas tries his best to fill Dick Sargent's shoes, but as he's playing a lion hunter with unconvincing hair extensions, many will not even recognize the homage.

Colonel John Patterson (Kilmer) gets off to a good start on the bridge, but work slows down when two lions begin hauling the workers away while they sleep, grabbing a fresh one before they've even finished the one they have. Their gluttonous behavior is puzzling and atypical— really something you'd expect from hyenas or brown bears. Aren't brown bears jerks, by the way? I don't mean to gossip, but even my zookeeper friends say they're getting sick of brown bears.

One of the locals names the lions The Ghost (after his great-grandma Theda Ghost) and The Darkness (which turned out to be the most popular lion name of the year.

All those people who named their killer lions The Darkness feel pretty foolish about it now). Patterson, who is under intense pressure to finish the bridge on time, shoots a lion and parades it before the men, who dutifully cheer. Unfortunately the dead lion was neither The Ghost nor The Darkness. It was simply Edward "Ed" Lion, who was out for a peaceful stroll, looking at the stars. The Darkness and The Ghost (The Darkness prefers top billing) continue to drag men away, just to be a-holes it would seem. Patterson's situation grows desperate. So desperate, in fact, that he allows Michael Douglas to be in his film.

Douglas plays Remington, a swaggering, half-crazy lion hunter who's supposed to be cool just 'cause he hangs out with Masai warriors. He and Patterson team up for a day hunt, which will turn out to be the first of their many countless failures to catch, shoot, hurt, insult, or even mildly annoy either The Ghost or The Darkness. Another failure begins when they force the workers to build a brand-new hospital, move all the patients there, then douse the old hospital with blood to lure the lions. It's a grisly version of something Yosemite Sam might have tried on Bugs. The Darkness and The Ghost talk it over, decide it's a trap, and raid the new hospital instead, killing dozens of recuperating patients and destroying hundreds of *In Style* magazines.

Remington, who looks progressively more like Dan Haggerty as the film goes on, suggests a plan in which a baboon is tied to a stake to try once again to lure the killers in. Everyone but the baboon agrees it's a good plan. It fails, of course, and all the baboon's family is left with are questions. Why? Why our baboon? Why not a douroucouli or a bonobo? What has our proud baboon family ever done to you? You can try to get the Remingtons and the Pattersons of the world to listen, but it's a long and bitter struggle, and one baboon family will not change the world.

There are other failures, one involving a large livetrap and some Muslim gunmen, and still another where Patterson straps on a pair of Acme Rocket Skates and chases the lions with a huge magnet.

Remington dies, which is fine because we had just about had enough of him, anyway, and Patterson finishes off the lions, The Ghost getting a long, self-indulgent death scene worthy of Captain Kirk's in *Star Trek Generations.*

In short, *The Ghost and the Darkness* is about as scary as an episode of *The Ghost and Mrs. Muir,* and Charles Nelson Reilly's performance looks nuanced and layered when compared with that of Michael Douglas's.

As for The Ghost, rumor has it he's fallen in with a bad lot and spends most of his film money at The Viper Room. The Darkness has distanced himself from The Ghost and is currently starring as Aslan in an off-Broadway production of *The Lion Won't Sleep Tonight,* a touching biography of the indefatigable King of Narnia. And Val Kilmer? No doubt he's being difficult somewhere.

THE EDGE

There's a bit of the survivalist in every male. You can see it in the steely gaze of a man who drives right by the Starbucks, testing his own mettle, hoping he can make it all the way to the office without a Mocha Almond Cappuccino with skim. There are men who push themselves, looking for their own limits, wondering if they can stand to wear their deck shoes without socks, even though it may dip into the fifties overnight. Every single man likes to think he would pass the ultimate test, that he still retains the steely core passed on to him by his rugged frontier ancestors. His deepest fear is that he's grown soft, by living soft and going easy on himself. He wonders if his Palm Pilot really makes him much of a man.

And so he plays golf. And installs a gas fireplace by himself, saving $87.50 in install fees. Sure, he smells gas the moment he turns it on, and the emergency visit from Tom at Riverside Plumbing and Heating costs nearly $300, but he tested himself—got outside his comfort zone.

This theme is at the core of *The Edge,* with Anthony Hopkins and Alec Baldwin. It's about men discovering just where their limits are, even while they run screaming from the biggest-ass bear you've ever seen.

Sir Anthony stars as Charles Morse, a jealous billionaire certain that his wife, a model, is having an affair with Bob, her photographer, played by Baldwin. A plane crash leaves Charles, Bob, and Bob's assistant, Stephen, stranded in the deepest wilderness, where they are soon pursued by a huge, smelly, slobbering bear, played by Daniel Baldwin (just kidding). They run around and yell at each other (the men, that is; the bear remains true to his kind and simply growls), saying very manly David Mamet-ian things to each other until before long Stephen gets munched down like a canapé. Don't get lost in the bear-infested woods with two guys who share top billing over you, is the lesson there.

Charles and Bob find themselves depending on one another and bonding in ways that a simple racquetball game never would have allowed. They sweat, and swear, and sharpen sticks, and it never even comes up that they're missing the Masters. They battle the foaming bruin with a woodsman's courage that does credit to their double-knit thermal polar fleece. The only manly thing they fail to do is grapple each other wearing nothing but jockstraps. (You men out there do, in fact, wrestle other men wearing nothing but jockstraps, right? Right, guys? I'm not alone here, am I?)

The part of Charles's wife is handled by Elle Macpherson, whose brilliant design for an automobile's front suspension does little to mitigate the fact that she's not a terribly good actress. My guy friends tell me that she's "hot." Well, so is the woman who gives me my towel at the health club, but she doesn't go around acting in bear movies all willy-nilly. It is really so difficult to see a beautiful woman these days that we need them clogging up our wild animal attack movies? Should we really be "looking" at them at all? What's wrong with our wives and girlfriends that we need to be taking up slots for actresses that might be slightly less hot to make room for nonactresses like Elle Macpherson (not to take anything away from her strut suspension design)?

In the end, *The Edge* is fairly successful within the genre of movies that feature wild animals attacking humans, among them *Jaws,* with the shark, of course; *The Ghost and the Darkness,* those killer lions; and *Sliver,* where William Baldwin goes after Sharon Stone.

I'm recommending it only for men, however, perhaps as a nice warm-up to a night of naked jockstrap wrestling.

MIGHTY JOE YOUNG

"The awesome and unpredictable forces of nature will not be controlled by man." This is the lesson Hollywood seems to want to teach us again and again. It must not be meant for me, however, because I personally have done nothing to try to control the awesome and unpredictable forces of nature, unless you count using my Weedwhacker. The theme seems to return again and again in countless monster movies from the '50s and '60s, in the classic *King Kong*, of course, and in *For the Boys,* where Bette Midler snaps her chains and goes on a rampage at a USO show, killing hundreds of GIs with her huge, powerful limbs.

It returned recently in the Disney remake of *Mighty Joe Young*, the 1949 classic featuring special effects by Willis O'Brien and Ray Harryhausen. Harryhausen would go on to make the remarkably stupid *Clash of the Titans*, which starred Harry Hamlin as a hot young lawyer battling armies of walking skeletons and trying to manage his sizzling office affair with the Gorgon Medusa.

Disney's update features Charlize Theron as Jill Young,

the woman who befriends a small, orphaned gorilla, and Bill Paxton as Gregg O'Hara, a conservationist who helps to protect the gorilla from evil poachers (as if all poachers are automatically "bad"). Paxton was actually first in line to play the role of Joe, the two-thousand-pound gorilla, convincing the director he could "do a De Niro" and pack on the weight himself. He even managed to grow a thick blanket of shiny black hair and was able to fish termites out of hollow logs using pieces of straw. It was only after he first "presented" and then charged the terrified director, flinging him like a rag doll, that he was shifted to the role of O'Hara.

The story begins with a prologue set twelve years in the past. Dr. Ruth Young, played by *Happy Days* alumnus Linda Purl, is killed by poachers, leaving her daughter, Jill, alone with Joe, the orphaned gorilla who, in a striking coincidence, shares the last name of Young. Ruth's last words to her daughter are, "Promise me you'll take care of Joe," not, "I love you," or even, "There's ham in the fridge, and remember you're going to Susan's after school."

We resume in the present to find conservationist O'Hara "conserving" the terrified gorilla by chasing it down with Humvees and firing blow darts into its head. Joe is now fully a one-ton gorilla, though not a single character in the movie is the slightest bit curious as to why or how he got to be so big. Is it just that postcollege weight that snuck up on him because he's not doing the intramural softball, and what with the new job it's just getting harder to find time to fit the running in? Is he pounding down can after can of Joe Weider Super Weight Gain Powder and washing it all down with Sports Shakes? My own theory is that he got one of those digital satellites and ordered the deluxe package. Now he just sits on his couch watching *Puppet Master III* and eating Red Baron Bacon Lovers Pizzas.

Eventually, O'Hara and Jill take Joe to a conservation park, where he can be more easily stolen by an evil poacher named Strasser (oh, let's just blame evil poachers for everything). Joe escapes from Strasser and begins a rampage at Palisades Park, riding the bumper cars twice without paying, not keeping his hands inside the cars at all times, shoving ahead of little kids for a place in line on the Wild Mouse. The police want to negotiate with Joe by pumping 3,600 rounds of ammunition into the great beast, but before they can, he saves a small, shrill child from a burning Ferris wheel and wins the hearts of everyone. I was a little disappointed it ended before I got to see him rough up the guy who runs the ringtoss concession.

If you must see a giant ape movie (and I can't imagine that you must, unless you have draconian state regulations), you'll probably want to see *King Kong* first. But if you're dying to see a Bill Paxton movie in which he stars with someone hairier and more inarticulate than himself, then *Mighty Joe Young* is your man.

DRAGONHEART

We live in an era bereft of true heroes. Our leaders are weak-willed and lack a moral core (I'm excluding Orrin Hatch, of course), and no matter how we try to imbue our sports stars and celebrities with even an atom of valor or fortitude, they let us down, either by injecting cattle steroids directly into their forearms or by attempting to take hostages at a Walgreens drugstore using an unloaded pellet gun. Let's face it, there's nothing mythic about Marky Mark, Skeet Ulrich, or Sarah Michelle Gellar. It's unlikely that Beck will display iron-willed courage when he can barely display those wispy, eighth-grade sideburns of his.

This dearth of actual gallantry, I believe, explains current interest in the ancient myths such as Arthur and the Knights of the Round Table, Hercules and his legendary journeys, and, from Sweden, Tåvold Jorgēnsēn and the Magic Sardines.

Dragonheart, starring Dennis Quaid and Sean Connery, celebrates the old ideals of chivalry, heroism, and hairy, odoriferous men in burlap underwear hitting each other with sharp things. It has much in common with Mel Gibson's *Braveheart,* the most obvious being the word "heart" in its title. This is a coincidence that cannot be ignored. I don't want to accuse either party of plagiarism, but some thieving bastard stole the whole "Blank-*heart*" idea from the other. It's not like "heart" is that common a word.

Putting my rage aside, I can tell you that *Dragonheart* tells the story of a knight named Bowen (Quaid), who is charged with teaching Einon, the frail son of the tyrannical king, the ways of the "Old Code" originated by King Arthur and his men many years before. When the king dies, Einon's first act as the new king is to receive a mortal wound after being gently bumped against a small wooden spike by a thin young girl, proving to his subjects that he's both very clumsy *and* a total puss. Einon's mother, Queen Aislinn, brings the dying puss to her neighbor, the fire-breathing dragon (voiced by Connery) for help. The dragon makes Einon promise that he'll follow the Old Code and then revives him by giving him half his heart, excluding his superior vena cava, which he quite likes and just can't bring himself to part with.

The resurrected Einon immediately becomes an even more corrupt king than his father, clearly illustrating that dragon-man heart transplants are not the miracle solution to corruption that they're always being sold as. Bowen assumes that Einon got a bad heart from the dragon, and so vows to destroy all dragons everywhere, except Daryl Dragon of The Captain and Tenille because he really liked the song "Do That to Me One More Time."

Bowen wipes out every dragon save the one he actually had the beef with. He calls a truce with him, names him Draco, and they team up to fight crime and corruption. It then becomes a buddy picture, paying obvious homage to *Tango and Cash* and *Perfect Strangers,* with Bowen in the Cousin Larry role and the Dragon as Balki.

The visual effect of Draco was achieved using the same technology as that used for *Jurassic Park,* wherein hundreds of supercomputers and thousands of man-hours are used to make the visuals look every bit as realistic as 1920s bendable clay puppet technology. Though animators admit they're not quite there, it does look as good or better than *Clutch Cargo* or even some of the *Gumby* episodes.

In the end, it's not a bad film, despite its weird message that a dragon with the voice of a craggy Scotsman died for our sins. I'm also uncomfortable with the new law that requires Sean Connery to appear in every motion picture released to the public. At least in this film he wasn't rubbing his ancient body all over some coquettish twenty-three-year-old *Dawson's Creek* alumnus. The Old-Guy-Beds-Young-Thing trend in Hollywood I find fairly repugnant. It's like watching a decrepit yak try to make love to a butterfly.

A featurette on the making of *Dragonheart* was included on the DVD version. Everyone involved gushed on and on about how much it meant and how close the project was to his heart. They seemed sincere, but it is, after all, *Dragonheart,* not a thirty-hour documentary on apartheid. You don't hear this kind of pompous self-importance from the people behind *Return to Gilligan's Island*.

Still, the film is an entertaining reminder that chivalry is an idea worth keeping alive. And, as such, it's really the only game in town, until they come out with *Tristan and Isolde* starring Katie Holmes and Beck.

It has long been theorized that DVD is the perfect medium for viewing bad snake movies starring Jon Voight, but until the release of *Anaconda,* it was only that: a theory. After one thorough viewing, I can happily report that if DVD is not the perfect medium for bad snake movies, it's pretty damn close!

Hollywood has been afraid to tackle the snake genre following the release of its masterpiece, 1973's *Sssssss* (pronounced "Ssssss." The last "s" is silent.) It took the complicity of former MTV V J Kari Wuhrer to get the project off the ground at all. Wuhrer, you'll recall, was the force behind 1991's *Beastmaster 2: Through the Portal of Time,* which was the prequel to *Beastmaster 3: The Eye of Braxus* (It was to be called *Beastmaster III: The Destruction of Jared Syn,* but producers panicked when they realized that was the title of *Metalstorm 2*!!).

The story of *Anaconda* begins when an anthropologist (Eric Stoltz) leads a film crew down the Amazon in search of a legendary tribe. Personally I would not put Eric Stoltz in charge of my lawn maintenance, but then that's why

I'm not backing anthropological expeditions. The trouble begins when they pick up a grimy, lubricious priest named Sarone (Jon Voight), who has adopted the accent of former Frito-Lay mascot the Frito Bandito. His menacing demeanor suggests a ruthless, cunning killer, but in a surprising twist, well, that's exactly what he turns out to be. The film couldn't quite manage the twist.

Voight, who is accustomed to working with large, slimy reptiles (he was in *Runaway Train,* with Eric Roberts), had better be careful or he'll end up in the Dennis Hopper/Jeremy Irons/Gary Busey bargain bin, playing nothing but psychos who taunt your Bruce Willis/ Sylvester Stallone/Kurt Russells through cell phones with lines like, "Tsk-tsk, Brannigan. We mustn't bring our nasty little gun, or people will *die*!" As it is, Voight chews so much scenery, you'd think he *was* Eric Roberts.

In *Anaconda,* it's Jennifer Lopez who lands the unpleasant job of having to deal with the huge, scaly creature. No one likes to act with Voight. (Yes! That's *two* nearly identical you-think-he-means-snake-but-he's-really-talking-about-an-actor jokes in *two* paragraphs. I am on *fire*!)

Stoltz landed the cushiest job as he is almost immediately stung in the throat by a large, aquatic wasp and spends the rest of the movie prostrate, with no more dialogue. It's a good job for an actor, a lot like doing *Whose Life Is It Anyway?* without all the strenuous talking. He was saved from having to give breath to much of the script, which is more an assemblage of random *words* than an actual *script*. It's of a declarative nature, mostly characters saying things like, "We need more fuel." Then, they go get more fuel. "That big snake is out there, somewhere." And, in fact, the big snake *is* out there, somewhere. It all makes for a special kind of tedium that would be impossible with a traditional, more "written" script.

Really, it's all just killing time until the huge digital snake encircles, consumes, and then regurgitates someone, a peculiar indignity that only certain actors can handle. For example, your Jon Voights and your Eric Stoltzes.

Suffice it to say that lots of people die, then the snake dies; along the way a few things blow up. The only question left to answer is this: Is the creature mentioned in the film, a kind of catfish that swims up the human urethra and digs its spines in, is this thing real? And if it is real, how does a creature like that evolve? Are there that many human urethras in the Amazon River?

Well, that's probably not what the producers wanted to leave me with.

The selling point of the whole thing, and the reason you spend the seventeen-dollar rental fee (late fees included), is the snake itself. And yet the shameful secret of *Anaconda* is how remarkably bad the digital snake really is. Newborns are not fooled by it. Ed Wood could do a better snake effect with a short length of clothesline and some Trilene. I've been more terrified of drain snakes (especially one wielded by a plumber who displayed what I thought was a particularly indulgent wedge of "bike rack").

So really, there's not a whole lot to the DVD, not even any nifty alternate audio track with the director explaining how he was able to make certain scenes as punishingly stupid as they were. As for digital snake movies as a whole,

I suggest alternate uses for the new ultrafast, liquid-cooled computers used to do the animation. Superviolent war games, or to order hard-to-find pen refills over the Internet, perhaps. How about a forty-foot-long digital Jon Voight?

ONCE BITTEN/ VAMPIRE IN BROOKLYN

Very little is known about Bram Stoker. Well, very little is known if you don't take the time to look up his name in the encyclopedia. If you work from memory, like I do, little is known beyond the fact that he wrote *Dracula,* and he was not in the movie *Stroker Ace.* Beyond that—a mystery.

Though my picture of him remains characteristically foggy, his legacy is clear. Not appearing in *Stroker Ace* took up almost no time for the great man. This left him many hours to write and direct his most famous works, like *The Apple Dumpling Gang* (based on a short story) and *Mrs. Doubtfire* (his most personal work). Despite his many accomplishments, people tend to remember him for *Dracula* (though I'll always remember him for inventing Mrs. Dash, a very decent-tasting salt substitute).

Clearly, *Nosferatu* remains a favorite. And people still applaud Bela Lugosi's nearly heroin-free performance in the Universal classic *Dracula.*

I recently viewed two films that cast doubts on Mr. Stoker's career. They are *Once Bitten,* staring Jim Carrey, and *Vampire in Brooklyn*, with Eddie Murphy and Angela Bassett.

As a serious film reviewer, I would be remiss if I didn't identify a bias toward Jim Carrey. I believe the world to be split into two camps: those who believe him to be a rubbery mock-up of Satan himself, an animated piece of refuse, a mephitic harlequin cast down by God to torment a weary world; and those who think he's "kind of funny."

Personally, I believe there is no hell foul enough to contain his fetid soul, though I admit I haven't seen *The Cable Guy*. And admittedly, there is a moment or two in *Once Bitten* where I didn't want to drive a fire ax into his chest, though my friends tell me I'm too charitable.

The plot of *Once Bitten* is as follows, and I quote. . . .

Lauren Hutton, star of *Gator*, is a vampire who needs the blood of a virgin to keep her young. Jim Carrey is a virgin trying to consummate his relationship with his girlfriend, a sane young woman who continually shoots him clean out of the saddle. Carrey, frustrated by his sensible squeeze, begins looking for someone who will touch his gummy being, a dilemma I can only assume echoes Carrey's real life.

What could be more repulsive than Jim Carrey "cruising for chicks"? Well, that would be Lauren Hutton taking him up on the offer. She drains his blood by piercing his inner thigh with her canines. (If that doesn't make you physically ill, you're no son of mine.)

Carrey begins behaving like a vampire, which worries his parents, who never think to ask him why he's thirty years old and still in high school. The rest of the movie is a struggle between Carrey's virginal girlfriend and the lycanthropic Hutton to win control of Carrey's body and soul. Fighting their own apathy, they do indeed struggle, and eventually Carrey lies with his Lady Love in a coffin, thwarting Hutton's evil plan. It's a touching bit of necrophilia that will have you snapping off the TV with tears in your eyes, gently holding your loved ones and weeping softly into the cruel night, pleading with some unseen guest, "Is there balm in Gilead?"

Vampire in Brooklyn is even better.

It's a more conventional vampire story that has yuck-meister Eddie Murphy (in cool hair extensions) playing an evil shape-shifter from the West Indies. He stows away on a ship bound for America, probably having gotten really tired of jerk chicken and steel drum bands. The ship crashes in Brooklyn, and Murphy immediately captures himself a "ghoul"— basically, an undead personal secretary who progressively rots over the course of the film. His septic body parts rotting and falling off is all played for laughs, and if you find yourself not laughing, well, then, you're probably well adjusted and in touch with your soul.

Angela Bassett portrays a cop trying to solve the grisly murders that Murphy perpetrates. The poor woman tries—I wanted to reach out to her, give her my counselor's number or send her a fruit basket—and though she lends a tiny sliver of dignity to the film, at heart it is a very ugly and dark work, and there is the dank smell of Murphy and his family members all over it. I found its treatment of women pretty reprehensible. Any woman portrayed as less than virginal is torn to pieces, vividly and graphically (though it's possible I'm seeing something that isn't there and I should just lighten up).

Also, the language is pretty rough. But provided you're a stable boy or a marine drill instructor, you shouldn't find it too offensive.

To sum up, I'm giving both these movies a thumbs-down, and urging you to run, run like the wind away from them!! Don't look back!!! For the love of god, RRRrruuunnnnnnnnnnnn!!*

*I apologize if my review seems ambiguous.

For those of you who were scared away by the abysmal reviews of *Batman & Robin,* let me lay to rest some of the prejudices you might have about the film. It's not the worst movie ever. No, indeed. It's the worst *thing* ever. Yes, it's the single worst thing that we as human beings have ever produced in *recorded* history. (There may have been a viler clay tablet somewhere in prehistory, but we mustn't spend time speculating on that.) *Batman & Robin* is an act of cold cynicism, reckless incompetence, and unbridled hate. It is a story filled with hints of fetishism and pederasty, displayed with a bald-faced contempt for its audience.

But, hey, that George Clooney is easy on the eyes, I'll tell you that for free!

The refreshing surprise of the movie was that Arnold Schwarzenegger *didn't* turn in the worst performance of the film. That distinction goes to Uma Thurman, who, as Poison Ivy, was as an irritant every bit as potent as her namesake. Jennifer Jason Leigh will be calling her for tips on how to be more grating. Chris O'Donnell turned in his usual performance, that is to say, none that I could see. He has all the screen charisma of a Timothy Van Patten. Alicia Silverstone's talents were exploited to the fullest, in that she wore a latex suit bedecked with rubber nipples (how I wish that were not true).

Yes, *Batman & Robin* boldly carried on the legacy of shame that began in 1989 with Tim Burton's masterfully unwatchable *Batman.*

Burton proved to the world what a shockingly over-rated director he was by helming a movie that succeeded solely on the brute-force power of the Hollywood hype machine. It is a dark, relentlessly boring, and utterly joy-less little film. It did, however, make for some fairly decent Happy Meals. The toys were colorful, the fries were crisp, and the burgers were refreshingly free of E. Coli–produc-ing animal feces.

Burton pulled off a nice trick in that he used almost no lights in the film, dispensing with the need to actually show the audience anything. With the actors obfuscated by utter blackness, Burton was free to not tell any kind of story or create any characters worth caring about, simply because *no one could see them*! He deserves credit for that, if for nothing else than his goofy hair.

Batman Returns (1992), for my money, runs neck and neck with *Batman & Robin* for utter loathsomeness. Danny DeVito, I think we can all agree, is the enemy of every-thing good and decent in this world, and *Batman Returns* is simply chock-full of the freakish little golem. Why anyone thought that the sight of DeVito ramming alewives into his twisted, purple maw was something to be projected onto a large screen for viewing by other human beings was a good idea, I'll never understand. It is a revolting thing, best seen on an empty stomach, and even then, best not seen at all. Unfortunately I had eaten sooner than eight days before my viewing of *Returns,* and my normally stable gorge threatened to rise more than once. Only the calming effect of a Pat Hingle performance could still my roiling system.

Batman Forever (1995) proved once and for all that the makers of *Batman*—namely Warner Bros., Tim Burton, and Burton's handpicked protégé, Joel Schumacher—despise all of humanity, actively work for the death of joy, and attempt to convince mostly impeccant children that the world is a black, violent, unstable place tottering precariously on the edge of unthinkable evil, their immortal souls in the hands of a lonely, basement-dwelling bachelor wearing a rubber codpiece. I'm guessing that at any one time in Los Angeles alone, there are hundreds of lonely, basement-dwelling men wearing rubber codpieces, but not for a minute do I believe that humanity is beholden to them in any way.

Batman Forever starred the allegedly pigheaded Val Kilmer, a mostly talent-free individual who has somehow gotten the opposite impression and therefore terrorizes movie sets with Kathleen Battle–like impertinence. Aside from filling out his Marquis de Sade Signature Collection leather and rubber jumpsuit, he really made no impression on me at all.

No despised film would be complete without the twisted Plasticine form of the Horned One himself, Jim

Carrey, and *Batman Returns* delivers *33 percent more Jim Carrey than our twelve-ounce size!*

Given my strong reaction, perhaps I'm not the audience for any of the *Batman* series. My guess is the perfect audience member is under eight. And drunk. And asleep. And a lover of all that is evil.

If you are, then, a narcoleptic, alcoholic seven-year-old, I can heartily recommend the *Batman* series entire!!

WILD THINGS

It is part of the common folklore that many of our greatest innovations started as downright mistakes. The most useful antibiotic in human history was discovered when Alexander Fleming dropped part of his tuna melt into a dish of streptococcus he had lying around. He was about to clean up the lab when his ride showed up to take him to his parents' place, where he stayed for the weekend. When he returned he noticed that the moldy bread had interfered with cell wall production in the streptococcus, and so he taunted them about it, calling them "stupid-ass streptococcus" and saying, "Can you produce cell walls now, huh?" Twelve years later, while Chain and Florey were commercially producing penicillin, Fleming was still laughing and high-fiving his research assistant.

Silly Putty, of course, came about when a highly paid R&D man was trying to pad his time card in order to buy a new pipe. The Twinkie, again a mistake, was created at the FermiLab particle accelerator facility while physicists were trying to isolate the radioisotopes of "creme filling" and "snack cake." Why, even Columbus thought he had sailed to India, the moron. He was probably so woozy on Amontillado and paella, his crew could have told him they were in Isabella's bedroom and he would have believed it.

This kind of happy accident can occur with films, as it did with *Road House*, still the greatest movie of its kind, and the more recent *Wild Things*. It's a delightfully stupid thriller starring Kevin Bacon, Matt Dillon, and Neve Campbell. Denise Richards's breasts, fresh from their triumphant performance in *Starship Troopers*, star as Kelly Van Ryan's breasts, which belong to a high school student who accuses handsome teacher Sam Lombardo (Dillon) of rape, a charge corroborated by Suzie Toller (Campbell), a trashy girl from a family of semiprofessional alligator wrestlers (the film left me with a highly unfavorable impression of semiprofessional alligator wrestlers, one that I hope will be remedied by the upcoming S.P.A.W.A.–sponsored feature *Jack McGraw: Semiprofessional Alligator Wrestler!*).

It turns into a tense courtroom drama, the viewer driven nearly mad with suspense wondering if Denise Richards will be able to wear a thong during the hearing. The plot will keep you on your toes, always guessing where the remote is, wondering if maybe you shouldn't get to that broken closet door you've been meaning to fix. And right when you're committed to doing just that, *one of the women peels off another layer of clothes!* You're trapped!

The best performance of the film comes from Robert Wagner, as Van Ryan's attorney. His line "You're through in this town, Lombardo. Take a hike," is the highlight of the film. Though he's good in this, and his wildly successful power painter has saved me countless hours of back-breaking labor, I have to admit I worry about his career in general. The *Hart to Hart* feature film has been shelved, maybe indefinitely, and George Hamilton is clearly in his way for other plum roles. I'm developing a showcase for him with my biopic of Bob Barker, but it's slow going, and I'm stuck on the scene depicting his historic meeting with Wink Martindale.

One caveat. Kevin Bacon plays Ray Duquette, one of the cops investigating the case. At one point, long after the viewer has been sedated by endless shots of taut midriffs and champagne-anointed breasts, Bacon unveils his own thick-cut peppered bacon, if you catch my meaning. I haven't been able to eat any smoked pork product since that moment. Just thought I'd warn you.

Some fans of the film will complain that my reviewing it as a "good-bad" film misses the intended satire, but to that I say, "Pah!" and even, "Nyeh!", perhaps a "Tcha!" I contend that making a film that is only part satire is hedging your bet, in a sense saying, "If you like it and think it's good, it's because it was a good thriller. If you think it stinks, then I meant it to be funny." It's a coward's way to make a movie, the kind of thing you'd expect from Cousin Larry before Balkie set him straight. Besides, we're talking about John McNaughton here, the director of *Henry: Portrait of a Serial Killer,* a film that flatly and graphically depicted the most heinous acts ever seen on-screen. It's like a Sinbad movie only with gore. He gets no slack from me. Face it, Mr. McNaughton, you made a lousy film that's so bad, it's funny.

It certainly is no *Road House,* mostly because it lacks the upright moral tone of that film. *Wild Things* does leave you feeling that while you're enjoying its camp appeal, somewhere there are other odorous, unkempt men enjoying it on less wholesome levels. If you're one of those men, my apologies. Enjoy the show.

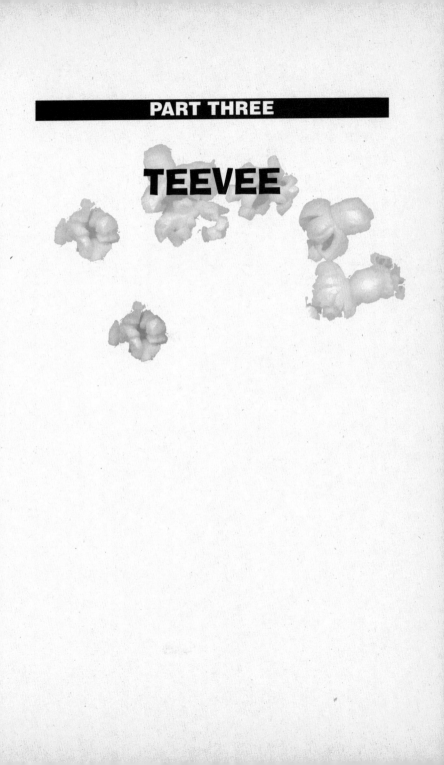

PART THREE

TEEVEE

BAYWATCH

I read recently that David Hasselhoff's nautical safety program *Baywatch* is viewed by as many as a billion people per week. Should we be at all concerned? Does this portend the end of time? Nostradamus predicted Hasselhoff's coming in his twenty-seventh quatrain, which reads, "A man with the legs of an egret will come from the west and many will follow him. Tan shall be his skin, and his gut will he suck in." Then the quatrain finishes by describing a piece of lumber with a red hat that will carry berries to a powerful monkey, but I didn't find that at all relevant, so I chose to leave it out. Frankly, I think the saturnine Frenchman pioneered the use of cannabis. Even as he roamed Europe, teaching people about the bubonic plague, he always had a huge bag of Chee•tos Paws.

The point is, there's nothing to worry about, and if *Baywatch* keeps half a million Germans off the street for an hour a week, I think everyone, especially people from neighboring countries, feels a little safer. (The European preoccupation with our *Hollywood Squares*–grade actors has always puzzled me. I picture French television as a medium populated with dark, moody films starring Donny Most and Bonnie Franklin.)

I myself have not watched the show since its halcyon days, when Nicole Eggert*, as "Summer," romanced real-life surfboard hero Kelly Slater. Slater tried, but the poor guy just couldn't act, and he always looked as though he had just taken a board to the back of the head. Consequently even Pamela Anderson acted circles around him. This was when Pamela was new to the show, and hadn't her trillion lonely GIF-downloading fans as yet. It may even have been before she had all her skin removed and replaced with easy-to-clean vinyl siding. The show was unselfconsciously stupid back then, full of a raw and ragged energy. Like the early days of *We Got It Made*.

My disenchantment with *Baywatch* has led me to other, more freshly moronic shows. I had a brief and bitter dalliance with *Thunder in Paradise*, the Terry "Hulk" Hogan–Chris Lemmon vehicle. Hogan and Lemmon gamboled about in tiny Speedos, the kind that make a nearly lifelong boxer-short wearer like myself shift uncomfortably in my seat. They cruised about in a huge super-high-tech boat, displaying their shiny, be-Naired bodies as they conquered drug dealers and gunrunners. In the end, I'm left mostly with the impression of Hogan's why-bother mustache. Small, blond, and barely perceptible, it sits mysteriously on his imposing head, appearing and disappearing as it shifts in and out of light and shadow. It's the

---

*Eggert cut her teeth on the Scott Baio/Willie Aames sitcom *Charles in Charge*. I liked *Charles*, though it was clear that the Aames-Baio chemistry that had been so evident in *Zapped!* was somewhat lacking.

Brigadoon of facial hair, and if you're unfamiliar with it, it can leave you with a vaguely uneasy feeling, as though you've left the iron on. Perhaps men like he, Martin Mull, and Ed Begley, Jr., look in the mirror and see Edward James Olmos–like mustaches, where the rest of us see only those pale, blond patches of fuzz.

I can't help but wonder whether Chris's dad, Jack Lemmon, ever visited the set of *Thunder in Paradise,* giving tips to his son. "Break down your script into beats to better chart your emotional growth, son. Oh, and shift your swimsuit, I can see the little sizzler."

I didn't last long with *Thunder,* so I was excited when the USA Network began running *Pacific Blue. Blue* stars Jim Davidson, Darlene Vogel, Marcos A. Ferraez, and Paula Trickey as police officers on bike patrol in a beach community. In order to enjoy it, it's important you get over your skepticism that there is intrigue in the world of bike patrol cops. Let go your image of them as doughy loners busting in-line skaters for going the wrong way on the bike path. Quell your impression of them as lackluster doughnut-vacuums sullenly enforcing leash laws. Overcome your belief that they're hostiley confiscating your Genuine Draft because of feelings of inferiority even when compared with meter maids, and you'll find a world of gorgeous women and buff hunks matching wits with criminally gorgeous women and nefarious buff hunks.

Its success gives me hope for the new show I'm developing. It's called *Hot Ice,* and it's the story of a group of sexy Sno-Kone salesmen who go undercover in the shady world of beach vendors. In the first episode they bust a

Dreamsicle salesman who's running a prostitution ring out of his cooler.

Competing with me is the already entrenched *Baywatch Nights,* obviously a spin-off of, well, *Baywatch,* the premise of which is that David Hasselhoff is a private eye on his downtime from lifeguarding who runs his business out of Lou Rawls's nightclub. This is a tougher Hasselhoff, a return to the almost *Knight Rider*–ish Hasselhoff of the '80s. A Hasselhoff who takes no guff from anyone, regardless of her cup size.

I'm told the new season will involve more of the supernatural: a fresh idea. I look forward to seeing poltergeists in thong bikinis, and those classic, onion-headed aliens flexing as sexy shape-shifters look on.

Actually, that gives me an idea. *Hot Ghosts.* It'll be a reality program that profiles the workouts, sex lives, and diet secrets of really cute apparitions. Or how about *Rescue 36–24–36?*

Perhaps I'll just become a hugely successful pop star in Germany.

THE FOOD NETWORK

Those who know me (and, as I get older, that number has dropped to about five) know that I like good food, provided there's lots of it. Skimp, and no matter how good the victuals, I just may tip the table over, David Banner–like, throwing open cabinet doors and shrieking article-free phrases like, "Me hungry more bird," and, "More potato. Three not 'nough."

Yes, I like food. When I'm not actually preparing, consuming, or thinking about foodstuffs, I'm watching programs about it on television. A sad confession, I realize, yet there must be others, for there now exists a network specifically for people like me—people who are basically hairless bears roaming the countryside looking for things to put into their heads.

It's called the Food Network, and that's not just titular. There really is a lot of food on the Food Network, often good food, which I should warn you can be a problem when you're watching someone prepare a couscous-crusted filet of salmon with jicama salad and crunchy basmati rice, and all you've got in the house is Polish mustard and some pretzel dust at the bottom of the bag. Keep a lot of sea bass, cilantro, and truffle oil on hand if you plan to watch with any regularity. From what I've seen so far, there are very few recipes that call for Chee•tos Paws.

Not that I've sat all day watching their network (all right, I have), but there are a few of the shows of which I've grown quite fond. *Dining Around* is pleasant enough, and worth a look, provided it's not taking you away from your position as an anesthesiologist at St. Mary's. If, however, your responsibilities are somewhat less weighty, like mine, you can waste a half hour watching the two hosts, Alan Richman and Nina Griscom, visit restaurants that wouldn't think twice about letting me in (that's a good thing), and discuss food topics. No, this is not CNN, but I think if we were all honest with ourselves, we'd discover we'd rather hear about a nice pepper steak or a good brisket than the events in Zaire.

One caveat: Most of the restaurants they visit are in and around New York City. If, like myself and most of the country, you don't live in and around New York City, you'll have to make do with the restaurants you have in your area. For me that means pretending the scalloped potatoes at Denny's are roasted fennel bulbs from some oppressively hip eatery in SoHo.

I'm also fond of *Too Hot Tamales,* with chefs Mary Sue Milliken and Susan Feniger, an unlikely pair who offer up Southwestern recipes. The entertainment comes not only from the recipes but from the disparate nature of the two hosts. As you might guess, Mary Sue Milliken is tall and blond and looks as though she'd be more at home cooking cream of mushroom soup–laden casseroles than

Manchelementes with Arroz and Conchinita Pibil. Susan Feniger, on the other hand, has an accent that hints at connections to the cement industry, of guys who can "do a job for ya" if need be. They seem to get along fine, though now and again I sense that Susan has the urge to jack Mary Sue with her nutmeg grater.

As you waste ever more hours, why not take a look at *Molto Mario,* with chef Mario Batali. A stout, ponytailed fellow with a strict agenda of adherence to Italian tradition, Mario offers recipes like *Linguine Fine with Alici* and *Culingiones con Cirruba.* His discussions of the history of the dishes are interesting, though I get the feeling that non-adherence to the sometimes draconian rules of Tuscan cuisine would bring swift retribution from Mario's and Susan's friends driving dark, late-model American cars.

Now your day is blown—might as well stick around for *Taste,* with David Rosengarten. Here, Mr. Rosengarten takes one basic dish and explains the hell out of it. Personally I like that, and I like him. But I will admit it's not for everyone. A full thirty minutes devoted to recipes for, and the minutiae of, the matzo ball may send some viewers running to *The Man Show,* or that unearthly mess that stars Jenna Elfman (whoever she is).

Though I'm not a huge fan, I should mention the show *Gourmet Getaways,* with our old friend Robin Leach. It's pretty much what you'd expect, though Robin seems a little down on his luck these days. Now, instead of gadding about in the castles of Europe, Robin's thumbing his way to Phoenix, meeting that guy from *The Nanny* for lunch. Still, he's working.

There is one break-out star from the whole affair, one

Emeril Lagasse, chef and host of *The Essence of Emeril* and *Emeril Live*. People seem to like him because he utters phrases like, "kick it up a notch" and, inexplicably, "bam." Though I'm not immune to the charms of catchphrases (I still make my friends laugh with "sock it to me"), I have to admit, after the first 3,700 times, "bam" begins to get annoying. His irritation factor is somewhere between that has-been extreme sportster Dan Cortez and, well, Jim Carrey.

Though *The Essence of Emeril* is pretty tame fare, it's *Emeril Live* where he really gets to "kick it up a notch." You can "bet your bippy" the audience is entertained, though it leaves me wondering, "Where's the beef?" He makes constant references to David Letterman and queries the audience over and over, "Isn't this better than those other late-night shows?" Hmmm . . .

A sample of his crowd rap:

"Where you from?"

"New Jersey."

"New Jersey, huh? That's great. Stick around, 'cause we're gonna kick it up a notch."

Bam! That's what I say! Emeril aside, there are reasons to watch the Food Network. So, hey, all you "space cadets," "show me the money" and watch for the Food Network, 'cause, after all, "life is like a box of chocolates," right?

Right?

SAVANNAH

I live in the Midwest, and during the cold winter months there's really nothing to do but fall through the ice, or stay at home and watch Aaron Spelling–produced television shows. Let's face it, the withered, ropy little man is the King of TV. His pioneering efforts have given us *Robin's Hoods, Beverly Hills 90210,* and, of course, *Charlie's Angels.* When he's not adding on to the huge, hellish monstrosity that is his home, he's making another thirty gajillion dollars off of colorful shows that feature mostly pretty people who don't find work anywhere else. Well, anywhere but made-for-TV movies with titles like *A Stranger at Love Junction,* or *My Daughter's a Dancer: The Shannon DeLonglis Story,* or *Kiss Me, Kill Me.*

I'd better stop—I could do these all day.

Okay, a couple more. How about *She Walks with Lust,* or *Deadly in Pink: The Story of the Lingerie Killer.* Special bonus title: *Reluctant Centerfold: Nude Without Permission.*

But back to Spelling. Currently he's riding a high that includes *Melrose Place,* perhaps the most popular show in the history of the world, right behind the ongoing cracker saga *The Dukes of Hazzard* (poor Denver Pyle), and one of my favorites, *Savannah.*

I recently had the chance to see both, and I have to say, for my money, *Savannah* wins hands down. Give yourself a pat on the back, Mr. Spelling, and while you're at it, cut down several hundred acres of old-growth virgin white pine to build an addition on your hot tub! You've earned it.

I personally had thought that *Savannah* was a place of seduction and betrayal, a playground of the rich and soon-to-be rich. I thought it was a tangled web, was Aaron Spelling's *Savannah.* But according to the press release from the aged, sinewy duke of soap, Savannah "... is a world where traditions and bloodlines run deep. A world where passion and privilege collide."

I am deeply sorry for my error.

It stars David Gail, Beth Toussaint, George Eads, Jamie Luner, Robyn Lively, Paul Satterfield, Ray Wise, and if that's not enough, Shannon Sturges, whose grandfather was the legendary writer-director Preston Sturges.

The pedigree for all of them is impressive. Just listen to some of the *actual* movies and television shows that these people have been a part of: *The Return of Hunter. Green Dolphin Street. Blackmail. Lady Boss. Nightmare Café. The Ultimate Lie. Growing Pains. Diagnosis Murder. To Sell a Child. Why My Daughter? Rules of Marriage. Confessions of a Sorority Girl. Tryst. Less Than Perfect Daughter. Teen Witch. Hotel Malibu. Danielle Steel's Family Album. Liz: The Elizabeth Taylor Story. Fire in the Dark. The Taking of Flight 847. Desire and Hell at Sunset Motel.* And finally, *Mr. Write.*

My personal favorites from the above list: *Why My Daughter?* (which, if you didn't know the story, would sound like a particularly whiny plea) and *Mr. Write*, a heartbreaking biography of the little round-headed guy on the sides of Bic pens.

Given their experience, *Savannah* should be the ultimate nighttime soap, and so it is. If so, why is *Melrose Place* riding such an unchallenged high of popularity? It's more self-consciously wretched than the pure, snowy wretchedness that is Aaron Spelling's *Savannah*. Plus it's got Ray Wise, the poor man's Edward Albert. Or is Edward Albert the poor man's Ray Wise? I suppose it doesn't matter—I just like the guy. I hope he's making a billion dollars.

This lopsidedness is evident when one surfs the Infobahn, hungry for information on the latest Spelling offering. (If in fact you are surfing the Infobahn for information on Spelling shows, it's time for some good Adlerian therapy. I am currently seeing the very sympathetic Dr. Rimbaud, who assures me that we can taper the sessions back to six a week provided I don't say the words "Courtney Thorne-Smith" for the next month.) Anyway, when you log on, it quickly becomes evident that people all over the world are talking about Aaron Spelling's *Melrose Place* and giving Aaron Spelling's *Savannah* short shrift! How do you think this makes Aaron feel? Not very good, I suggest. Do you realize how many rooms he has to build on the South Wing to begin to stanch the wound? Can you picture the poor, towheaded sleaze-master bent, weeping on his daughter's hideous plastic chest? Just picture that scene and try to freeze him out.

What I'm saying is, open your heart to another

Spelling show. Say you're already watching *Beverly Hills 90210* and *Melrose Place*. Even given your steady diet of Must-See TV, it's really not that much more of an effort to catch *Savannah*.

Perhaps I can hook you.

On the episode I just saw, Lane, played by Robyn Lively, was to marry, I don't know, one of those dopey-looking guys. To me they're all the same, with those monstrous jaws and too much cartilage. They all resemble those freshly shaved guys on razor commercials who have anonymous women rise up and feel their chins.

Anyway, the diminutive Lane is to marry one of these chunks, but she misses her own wedding because she downs enough straight vodka and pills to keep Reggie White as stoned as Robert Downey, Jr., for a decade. Meanwhile, there's sleazy politics going on with Ray Wise, there's affairs and evil twins—in short, the entire color-ful, yet extremely limited palette that Spelling has at his disposal.

Please tune in. If only to keep the palette loads of skin bronzer coming to Aaron's beloved Tori.

I leave you now with a few more suggestions for made-for-TV movie titles.

The Naked Killer. I Drink Till I'm Nude. Deadly Buttocks. Savage Panties: The Story of the Victoria's Secret Murders. Ten Who Spank.

And finally, *Not Without My Swimsuit.*

Note to producers: You have my permission to use any and all of these titles. I'd consider it an honor.

JUDGE JUDY

I've never been one for reality-based programming, unless you count the James Brolin–Connie Sellecca series *Hotel,* a searing account of actual romance and intrigue, taken from court transcripts, I believe. But beyond that and the occasional celebrity trapshoot show, the only one I've watched with anything more than unhealthy regularity is *The People's Court.* The endlessly sagacious Judge Wapner ruled his court like, well, like an old, cranky guy. Sort of like a silver-haired Bob Dole without the charm. The dime-store Solomon presided over such gut-wrenching legal battles as The Case of the Returned Moccasin, and The Faulty Dental Floss. It was either a glorious end to a distinguished career, or a shameless grab for some easy green before slipping into a pair of boxer shorts and tottering around his apartment for ten or twenty years drinking from a bottle of Cabinstill.

Wapner was a granite tower of dignity compared to the very hittable Doug Llewelyn. He looked a little like Franken Berry the cereal mascot, only with Wink Martindale's hair. A black hole from which no charisma could escape, Llewelyn would collar peeved pet owners and dissatisfied blanket buyers as they left the "court." As if their lives weren't bad enough, forced to air the sad details of their existence in front of millions just for a sliver of recognition and a chance to recoup the thirty-three dollars lost on The Broken Hair Dryer, the people then had to be worked over by this cadaverous ur-man.

Yet somehow it all worked, and bazillions of people tuned in on a daily basis, I among them. Though I have an excuse (I have no life), I suspect its popularity was based on the fact that were we not watching this, we might be forced to endure one of the hundreds of Michael J. Fox movies released weekly throughout the entire decade of the '80s.

The People's Court exists in reruns, yet to actually *watch* said reruns of *The People's Court* is to give up on life and hope. Indeed, to spend any more time with Llewelyn is to turn your back on grace and love, to deny the existence of beauty. But if you do want to see it, check your local listing.

For those thirsting for even more intrigue from the paneled halls of justice, there is terrific news: *Judge Judy*! This show, too, is baked fresh from the monstrous kitchens of Doug Lewellyn, who shows a tiny shred of decency by not appearing on-camera. This is Judy's show. Judge Judy dispenses wisdom and mercy from behind a tall, suitably judicial desk that looks over a brown room, done in trailer-park motif, much like Wapner's domain. She purrs and rages, condemns and comforts, hurling psychic lightning bolts on all who would evade her piercing questions on "just what happened when you bought the slippers." She's like a mean Nancy Culp.

On the episode I just watched, J. J. frothed at some poor, greasy, ponytailed polygamist and his seven teenage wives (frightening creatures, none with even a speck of pigmentation. Very strange). The oily carnival worker did his best, spewing specious logic and very tenuous sophistry, but little of it was heard over Judge Judy's pointless yelling. She likes to yell a lot, from what I can see. She reminds me of the people you see behind the thick glass at the impound lot, or staring at you over the unemployment office counter (where I've worn the carpet bare, by the way). Though I'm sure that yelling has its place in the criminal justice system, as witnessed by the dozens of hair-trigger cops who've collared me for parking violations, I think at Judy's level the yelling should be tempered with an atom or two of actual adjudicating, or perhaps a grain of wisdom. If not, you're no better than my uncle Wally, an angry, pink man who once stuck an old tooth back into its socket with chewing gum because he had a hot date with Yolanda (oh, how I wish that weren't God's truth). He always reminded me of a somewhat upright breeding hog.

Anyway, *Judge Judy*.

Judy got into a contretemps with one of the carny's bony wives over the law that allowed the slimy dope to marry her at the age of fourteen. It was a small blip of excitement in a half hour that was otherwise blipless, but even that was fairly wan and I found myself wishing that the sad Melissa Gilbert-ian woman would leap over Judy's desk and deliver a couple haymakers to her midsection before being coldcocked by one of Llewelyn's minions.

Though I risk being tracked down myself and hit by the honorable one, I have to wonder whether Judy isn't taking the easy way out, sniping at lubricious polygamists. It's not like anyone's going to disagree with her. Why doesn't she challenge herself and put Jimmy Carter on the stand? Accuse him of embezzlement and shoddy workmanship on his Habitat For Humanity homes? No, instead she high-handedly takes after a moist, corpulent man who undoubtedly will end up, shirtless and dazed, on *Cops*, being yanked out from a crawl space below his steps.

In the end, Judy dismissed her court without ever delivering a verdict, not that anyone seemed to care. She probably had to nip off to the airport to meet up with Wapner for a Carnival Cruise. She has a nice scam going.

If you want to see a more accurate replica of the criminal justice system, I suggest you spend a few hours with *Night Court*. Richard Moll is better looking, and Harry Anderson is easier to take than the stern, Margaret Hamilton of a woman who is Judge Judy.

HERCULES

In these dark and desperate times, when a Pauly Shore movie lurks moistly behind every corner, America is in desperate need of a hero. And that hero is here—*but does it have to be Kevin Sorbo?* 'Fraid so. This meaty, affable beefsteak of a man has come to kick butt and chew ambrosia—and he's all out of ambrosia. Sorbo stars as Hercules, the doofy demigod who, according to the legends of those original weirdos, the ancient Greeks, killed the Nemean Lion and the Hydra; captured the savage bull of King Minos of Crete; fetched the golden apples of Hesperides; and a bunch of other crap.

Frankly, I think each and every ancient Greek had a one-hitter stashed in his toga. I hope some stoner from our era sits down and, in a haze, writes down the legends of Pluthomene, who rode into Gasthamena and took the dreaded lock of Platheran from Galgothem in the time of Oisfkjin—*and then every single school kid two thousand years from now will have to read his cannabis-fueled ramblings day in and day out, a ruler poised over their tender knuckles just wait-*

ing to strike if they confuse the golden yahmanian with the fleece of Thartuniam!!!!!!

Sorry.

Hercules: The Legendary Journeys is part of the Universal Action Pack, a pack that used to include the Greg Evigan vehicle *Tek War*, based on the novel written by William Shatner. (*Written* by William Shatner. Yup, he wrote 'em. No doubt in my mind or anyone else's.) In my opinion, when the Action Pack was in full swing, it was quite comparable to a nice six-pack of Trappist Ale, or a good Doppel Bock, but now with *Tek War* gone, the Action Pack is like a half-finished six-pack of Red, White and Blue, or Red Grape Malt Duck.

But Hercules is extremely popular. Due, in large part, I think, to Kevin Sorbo, who to my eyes looks something like a mesomorphic Todd Rundgren, or perhaps a beefy Steve Perry, lead singer of Journey. Perhaps it's the hair, but he doesn't so much look like a hero bent on righting wrongs as he does a guy wearing animal print Zubaz cruising around Glendale in his van looking for used stereo gear.

Obviously this is part of the mission of the show, to update the legend; to make it palatable to men and women who shop for Joe Weider products at General Nutrition Center; to appeal to your average Joe at the mall buying a loaded baker over at One Potato Two; to keep the machinist in his chair drinking Mickey's Big Mouths for one full hour each week.

In this role, Sorbo excels. The ladies, and the guys, I'm told, seem to like him. There are hundreds of Web sites dedicated to him, he's on the cover of magazines, he's starring in an upcoming movie, and he was recently seen on the cover of *TV Guide,* looking every bit like he had just been panfried by Martin Yan.

I've never understood why you have to take a perfectly good muscle guy and cover him with canola oil. (All right, settle down. I meant it innocently enough.)

So does he live up to the hype? Well, he's not bad, and the show is entertaining enough, if you don't expect much at all. Say, if you like *Chicago Sons,* or *Nash Bridges.*

The knockout punch of the Action Pack comes with *Xena: Warrior Princess,* starring Lucy Lawless. It's a lot like *Hercules,* only with one notable difference: It's not Hercules and his sidekick traveling around New Zealand kicking people's butts; it's Xena and her sidekick traveling around New Zealand kicking people's butts! You see? How much more different could you get?

Again, they've found a perfectly appealing lead in Lawless. The men like her, and the ladies seem to like her, too. Me, I think she's wonderful but, right or wrong, I feel nervous around any woman who can bench-press me. This is not to deny Lawless her very obvious femininity. For me, it comes down to sheer practicality; I don't want to lose a fight over the remote control and have my mate pin me to the couch and dangle spit in my face until I promise to change it to *The Preacher's Wife,* even though I was in the middle of watching *McLintock!* for only the second time that night. (I realize the preceding paragraph only serves to illustrate the sad reality that most men believe deep down that all women, even those they see on television, are potential mates.)

My sad prejudices aside, *Xena* is an okay way to spend an hour, provided your expectations aren't too high. Say, if you like *Men Behaving Badly* or *Jag*.

Naturally the success of *Hercules: The Legendary Journeys* and *Xena: Warrior Princess* was bound to inspire others. My favorite copycat, or "otherly inspired" show is *The Adventures of Sinbad,* starring Zen Gesner, George Buza, Jacqueline Collen, Tim Progosh, Oris Erhuero, and other people with silly names. Zen Gesner is Sinbad, and again, he looks not so much like a mythical hero as he does Jack Wagner in a turban.

The premise is shaky to begin with. I mean, Sinbad is funny, and certainly he was great in such movies as *Houseguest* and *First Kid,* but basing an action series on him seems silly, especially when you've got a thin white guy named Zen Gesner playing him.

The press releases tell me that Zen Gesner was one of the first Americans to be admitted into the London Academy of Music and Dramatic Art. Oh, great—a man named Zen Gesner, who looks like Christopher Atkins without the pukka shells, is our ambassador in the hallowed halls of British stage acting. They send us Sir Anthony Hopkins; we give them an updated Lance Kerwin.

Still, we're shipping them episode after episode of silly action shows, and they're eating them up as though they were blood pudding or toad-in-the-hole or some other creamed organ meat with a silly name.

I say pass the spotted dick and turn on *Hercules*!

Like most white men my age, I find it difficult to make new friends. My wife, who has just over seventeen thousand close friends, suggests that I reach out to people. Frankly that seems a bit much. Sure, the guy who sold me tires was nice enough, but am I really going to ask him to go to a game with me? By the time he'd stop hitting me, our tenuous relationship would most likely be irreparably damaged. Plus, I'd still need tires.

Just keeping the old friends is becoming increasingly difficult as our paths diverge, and our common language shrinks to merely include the word "hey." And so my course is clear: to go through life pretending to have done and seen things that have *hardened* me—made me aloof and unreachable. Which works, until I need to ask a stock boy where they keep their corn meal. Then the facade crumbles, and it's clear that I'm not a weathered loner who's seen too much; just a pasty Midwesterner who can't find the flour aisle.

This dearth of real friends makes me the perfect viewer for NBC's *Friends,* a show so minutely targeted to my demographic that watching it and buying the sponsor's products seems like a mere formality. It's a foregone conclusion that I'll be warmed by the gentle wit of Chandler, the earnestness of Ross, and the occasional bra-lessness of Rachel. And yet, it leaves me cold. Yes, everyone on it is nice looking, pleasant, and mildly amusing. But if that's all I want, I can go to the lumberyard. I think the people pulling the strings at NBC underestimated how aloof and hardened by life I've become.

Given this predisposition, I did not expect to like either of the romantic comedies with "Fool" in the title starring guys from *Friends*: Matthew Perry's *Fools Rush In* or David Schwimmer's *Kissing a Fool*. And I didn't, really, though it's not specifically the fault of either actor. Each was as likable and charming as anyone at the lumberyard. Or my tire salesman, for that matter.

Fools Rush In is the story of a slick New York City professional (Perry) sent to Las Vegas to oversee the construction of a nightclub, who meets and promptly sleeps with a Mexican-American cigarette girl, played by Salma Hayek. He soon learns that there are consequences to sleeping with Mexican-American cigarette girls played by Salma Hayek, namely children and marriage, things synonymous with career suicide to slick New York City nightclub-construction overseers.

Perry and Hayek are charming enough, as it goes. The problem is that the whole movie is written and directed about as artfully as a Tums commercial. Sure, there've been Tums commercials that are effective enough in conveying the relative acid neutralization capabilities of the product, but on the whole it's a pretty dry business. The little Tums-shaped sponge soaking up a liquid meant to represent stomach acid? Well done. But not really artfully done. The *Dragnet*-style singing of "*Tums,* tums tums tums, Tums"? Nice. But, again, nothing to write home about. So it is with *Fools Rush In.* They soaked up the stomach acid nicely, but they didn't give me my daily allowance of calcium, if you know what I mean.

Though *Kissing a Fool,* starring Schwimmer as a roguish and popular TV sportcaster, is not much better than, say, a Dodge truck commercial, or an Applebee's ad, it isn't his fault. No, the fault lies almost entirely with Jason Lee, starring as David Schwimmer's friend. Lee, who was also in *Mallrats* and *Chasing Amy,* allows Schwimmer to blow him not only off the screen but out through the lobby and into the karate school next door. I mean this in the nicest way, intending not to offend but rather for the purpose of elucidation, and any unkindness that the reader infers is not calculated on my part, but Jason Lee sucks more than you can possibly imagine. He sucks out loud. He sucks on toast. He forces me to use the word "sucks," a term I normally find mildly abhorrent, simply because he sucks. His suckiness is thorough, diligent, and complete. He is to be congratulated for the sheer depth of his suckation. Again, this is meant as criticism, not to impugn his character. I can't even begin to imagine him sucking this badly in other areas of his life.

Man, he sucked.

Schwimmer wasn't bad, though. And neither was Bonnie Hunt, or Mili Avital as Schwimmer's, and then Lee's fiancée. A nice, appealing little project *until they dropped a rotting squirrel carcass named Jason Lee right into the punch bowl!*

I have again forgotten my wife's advice: "Fewer rotting squirrel carcass analogies equals more friends." I suppose it's too late to see if Jason Lee wants to go to a game with me.

THE CARTOON NETWORK

Ted Turner makes more money rolling over in bed than the states that border Canada do all year long. After making eighty bajillion dollars ruthlessly crushing competitors and casually ordering the deaths of hundreds of small business employees (though I have no proof of this), Turner glorified himself by giving a tiny portion of the money, taken directly from the hands of hungry, big-eyed children, to the United Nations. At the rate their fortunes are being amassed, in several years Bill Gates and Ted Turner will simply do "halfsies" with the planet Earth. The Sun and the planets of our solar system will be divided up in the codicil of the contract for some mutually agreed upon, etc., etc. Truth be told, I wouldn't mind seeing Gates and Turner slug it out in a no-holds-barred cage match. Each would be given a leather jock-strap, some body oil, and a folding chair, and . . . well, I've strayed far afield of my main point.

The point is, part of Turner's huge sovereign empire, an empire akin to Sauron's from *The Lord of the Rings,* was built with the dollars made off of a fairly entertaining little cable station known as The Cartoon Network. Though Turner has largely failed in his attempt to buy a great baseball team (beaten by the Minnesota Twins?!), and though no amount of yachting or marrying Jane Fondas will convince us he wasn't a geek in high school, it must be admitted that he's good at building cable networks.

I can't imagine Turner is a huge cartoon fan, yet it's fun to imagine him and Jane sitting at home in their tattered sweats, eating mustard-flavored pretzels and coughing 7Up out their noses after seeing a particularly funny *Scooby-Doo*.

What can you find on The Cartoon Network? Well, unfortunately, it does rely fairly heavily on reruns of the *Scooby-Doo* series, one of the dumbest things man has ever produced. It's not funny, it's horribly repetitive, and the animation makes *Clutch Cargo* look like *Wallace & Gromit*. But it does have the distinction of having foul-mouthed Top 40 peddler Casey Kasem as the voice of Shaggy! That said, it must be noted that *Scooby-Doo* is much better than the spin-off, *Scrappy-Doo,* featuring Scooby's nephew. Compared to that, *Deputy Dawg* is a work of unbounded genius.

TCN also carries *The Flintstones,* the oeuvre of which has entered the canon of essential local television broadcast. *The Flintstones* isn't necessarily funny, but it's not the worst thing ever produced, that is, until you see the episode with that weird, big-headed Martian, the Great Kazoo, or Doodoo or whatever his name is. He is a hellish creation, irritating, possessive of a creepy patina that rivals that of the King of Creepiness, Dr. Smith from *Lost in Space.* Avoid that Great Wazoo at all costs, lest you have nightmares of a little green Ross Perot in a cape flying about your room.

If you can't get enough of *The Flintstones,* and there is frankly no scenario that I can imagine where you couldn't, you can always try its sister show, *The Jetsons.* They are essentially the same show, featuring the same oddly drawn Hanna-Barbera characters—all big-nosed and ill-defined, the women tiny-waisted and dangerously thin, the men thick and misshapen from eating Bronto Burgers or Future Dogs or whatever the heck they are. The Hanna-Barbera take on the world is the same, too. The women are shrill, money-grubbing gossips, and the men are all dim-witted connivers who like meat. The corporate world is full of sawed-off, petty tyrants who live to torture their charges. The employees are spineless, waxen little men grabbing for a pitiable scrap of corporate leftovers.

In that respect, the show is refreshingly authentic.

As a tonic to that, why not try the Japanese phenomenon *Speed Racer.* (Not to spoil it for you, but Racer X is actually Speed's brother!) *Speed Racer* was probably the first successful Japanese import—long before Pink Lady, or tempeh, or imitation crab legs. Again, *Speed's* not funny, and it really has poor animation. In fact, it's not so much animation as it is drawings shown to you briskly while being acted out by community theater rejects who like to grunt a lot. Here's a little tip: I once dated a woman from Japan who told me that in her native country, the *Speed* song actually goes, "Mahi go go, Mahi go go, mahi go go go." Enjoy!

I urge you to avoid what one might consider the basement of The Cartoon Network. You're on fairly high ground with the Warner Bros. canon entire, and you'll have some fun with *Space Ghost,* an odd, entertaining little show, but stay away from *The Smurfs,* an entire hour of which airs every weekday morning. Smurfs do no one any good. Save providing '80s stand-up comedians with lame material, or entertaining a child under the age of four months, I can't see any reason for *The Smurfs* at all. Perhaps subhuman species might like them. Turtles or perhaps brown bears might enjoy *The Smurfs.*

Stay away from *Jabberjaw* as well. *Jabberjaw* is a great white shark with a voice like Curly from *The Three Stooges.* That's an odd concept, I don't care where you're from. That makes *H. R. Pufnstuf* look staid.

And proceed with caution when viewing *Woody Woodpecker.* He's a shockingly annoying character, and far from sympathizing with his acts of torment, you're left hoping he's beheaded, plucked, and roasted with chestnuts and fresh sage.

Avoid *The Pink Panther* altogether, unless you're a huge Pat Harrington fan.

These caveats aside, The Cartoon Network can provide distraction until the Gates-Turner cage match can be arranged. I think I'll call Don King tomorrow, see if Jane wants to throw in, too. Then, once the glasses and yachting caps start flying, we the American public can be truly entertained.

THE THREE STOOGES

Kurt Vonnegut talks with great fondness about the funniest thing he's ever seen: a bus door opening and a man in midfall coming out the door, his body horizontal to the ground. As far as I'm concerned, that's a tacit endorsement—from a pretty heady source, mind you—of *The Three Stooges*. The endorsements are necessary, I find, to defend my affection for what might possibly be the stupidest act ever to be exposed to film. (The reader is, I assume, making the Jim Carrey exception in his own mind. If we can't proceed with the common belief that Jim Carrey is a hideous rubbery reptile, sent as a messenger from Satan himself, then we have nothing in common.)

For what the august Mr. Vonnegut is saying is that seeing people in physical pain can be damn funny. This is not to say that seeing a man's head being forced into the spinning blade of a table saw is, by itself, funny (unless the man were Jim Carrey, of course). No. Certainly not. But if that man is named Curly, and if after skull meets saw blade the blade is bent at odd angles and the man named Curly laughs and points at said blade, well, then, we're talking comedy gold, in my opinion.

I'm defensive about the Stooges because I feel, as a person who generally abhors violence on television and in films, the Stooges are largely indefensible. Taken at face value, it's three men knocking the crap out of each other, with crowbars and monkey wrenches or anything that's handy. And though it's hard to explain the difference between a man's head being crushed in a vise in the movie *Casino,* and Shemp's head being crushed in a vise on the Stooges, a difference does exist, and morally, the victory goes to the "Oh, wise guy, eh?" and not the Wiseguys.

This all comes to the surface now because the Three Stooges are currently enjoying something of a renaissance on the Family Channel, and I'm sure there are many parents out there who are concerned about their children seeing harsh men in bowl cuts and shaved heads crushing the cartilage in each other's noses with pliers. As one raised on a steady diet of Stooges, I humbly offer myself as an example of what can become of a child exposed to their particular brand of violence: For five years, I talked to puppets on a daily basis. See? I'm fine.

As is so often the case, the responsibility rests with the parents. I think it's important for the father to point out to the child that using a crowbar to extract his friend's head from a mine shaft is a touchy business, one best left to Moe. It's the mother's job to explain that Larry has spontaneously regenerating hair, and if Moe grabs a generous handful and extracts it, it's okay because Mr. Fine can make more. Talk to your children, parents. Explain that Curly's head is at least as hard as industrial-grade diamonds and can withstand a thousand beatings by a thousand copper pipes without the least damage to his prodigious intellect.

I fear that parents will be swayed by watchdog groups who would have the Stooges suffer the same fate as Popeye. The last time I saw the poor, balding, bulbous tar was in a batch of nonviolent cartoons—he and Bluto working together to solve environmental issues, or some such thing. I wept for days. Even after viewing several Warner Bros. cartoons featuring Daffy Duck getting his beak blown clean off his face, I remained disconsolate. Only the sight of Curly, with childlike trust, hitting Moe's balled fist, then Moe pinwheeling his arm and sending that fist crashing onto Curly's bald pate, could cheer me in the least.

Another Stooge issue that must be faced before we can begin enjoying them without fear is the whole men-love-them–women-hate-them myth. I tire of this argument. True, I've never met a man who *didn't like* the Three Stooges. And though, true, I've never personally met a woman who *did like* the Three Stooges, we must remind ourselves that this is based only on thirty-two years of anecdotal evidence. And though it may further be true that I've never even *heard* of a woman who likes the Three Stooges, we mustn't be swayed by such hogwash. Certainly there are many studies that show that men and women love the Three Stooges equally. All we need do is find evidence of these studies, collect the data, publish it, and put to bed forever the horrible misconceptions that pullulate around the Three Stooges gender-gap issue.

Besides, I'm sure I need not remind readers of the violent subject matter of so many of the books, television shows, and movies that are generally considered to be for women. The fact that I can't think of a single one should not be held against me.

We need the Three Stooges, if only to remind us that, well, men hit each other with alarming frequency. Whether good or bad, it's true. Yes, men have in the past, and will continue in the future, to bend back the blade of a common carpenter's saw and sproing it violently into the face of other men. It's a truth that must be spoken of. And where else are you going to hear it? The films of François Truffaut? Preston Sturges? Laurel and Hardy? Okay, bad example.

We live in a world that has laid untold riches at the feet of Keanu Reeves as reward for his ability to say the word "whoa." A world where people do the bidding of Adam Sandler, gladly and without question, simply because he does a funny baby voice. And yes, horrifying as it may seem, Jim Carrey, our top box-office draw, feels free to speak out of his buttocks in front of a billion people on the Academy Awards.

I know you didn't ask, but can't there be room for me to enjoy the Three Stooges without guilt?

PART FOUR

SCIENCE FRICTION

LOST IN SPACE

It has become quite clear that DVD is the preeminent entertainment storage medium, just barely edging out "the backs of cereal boxes" in a consumer poll. And now, with the ready availability of DVDs over the Internet, it becomes even easier to rent incomprehensible Japanimation or the films of Jon Cryer. There are no excuses anymore. Everyone must be entertained at all times!

I shall always have fondness for the Internet DVD rental service that allowed me to see *Lost in Space* without having to approach a counter and say to another human being, "I'd like to rent *Lost in Space*." In general, it's unwise to be seen renting any Matt LeBlanc movie, especially if you have aspirations to run for some sort of public office. And given recent performances, it's become somewhat scandalous to consider renting Gary Oldman movies as well. If you must rent one, be prepared, if pressed, to say, "Oh, *that's* Gary Oldman! I was thinking of Daniel Day-Lewis."

Lost in Space is, of course, based on the Irwin Allen television show from the '60s that starred Billy Mumy and Jonathan Harris. It was the story of a creepy, mincing British man and his tenuous friendship with an earnest, unappealing boy . . . in space, I think. There might have been more to it than that; I never had the stomach to get through a whole episode, myself. It left me feeling strange and unsettled, as though someone had just dragged something dead through my living room. And Dr. Smith's alliterative tirades just left me feeling headachy and depressed. Perhaps this disqualifies me as an impartial critic of the film version.

No. I'm going to assume that they were going for that effect and that I'm actually a typical viewer. I shall press on.

As an initial point of comparison, I'd say the film version is somewhat like a fairly discreet sausage burp: It's somewhat reminiscent of the original yet not altogether welcome. It's too late to ask "why?" a *Lost in Space feature,* for we now know that such remakes are compulsory entertainment, and it shouldn't be long before we see Sarah Michelle Gellar as Tootie in *The Facts of Life: The Motion Picture.*

There's not much plot in *Lost in Space* that isn't described in the title. Matt LeBlanc, fresh from the triumph that was *Ed,* plays a hotshot fighter pilot who is ordered to escort a family to the other side of the galaxy to build some sort of a time gate, or some such thing. Frankly I don't pay much attention when they start dispensing the sci-fi mumbo jumbo. It all starts to sound like warmed-over *Stargate* to me. Anyway, Gary Oldman, as Dr. Smith, helps fulfill the promise of the title by sabotaging their ship and then stowing away on said ship in a clumsy maneuver reminiscent of Bob Denver in *Far Out Space Nuts* (the last sci-fi I liked, by the way).

The somnambulistic William Hurt plays John Robinson, patriarch of Clan Robinson, who is asked to endure the skull-crushingly annoying performance of Lacey Chabert as Penny Robinson. She's kind of the female Urkel, except that she has a pet digital monkey. Aside from being a tool to sell drink cups at KFC, there is no discernible reason to have a digital monkey in the film. Until! Aha, the DVD's helpful Special Features includes deleted scenes. Watch those and you soon discover—there was *really* no reason to have a digital monkey in the film. It's not even a *good* digital monkey. Donkey Kong, now *he* was a good digital monkey.

Fans of the original series (Are there any? Really? Put aside the camp appeal and answer me honestly.) will recognize cast members Marta Kristen, Angela Cartwright, Mark Goddard, and June Lockhart in bit parts. They won't *enjoy* them, because their parts are too small, but they will recognize them, if they haven't slipped out for bulk Gummi Worms. Conspicuously absent from the film is Jonathan Harris. Word on the street is that he demanded too much money for his participation. My theory is that he didn't have the energy to change out of his stained housecoat and turn off the reruns of *The Joker's Wild* on the Game Show Network.

As far as DVDs go, the *Lost in Space* interface is pretty darned good, and there are plenty of neat extras. Some sort of inverse law is at work here, for the same was true of the latest Carrot Top film. Not a darn thing on my copy of *Double Indemnity*, and yet *Father of the Bride Part II* probably bristles with extra features and artfully shot documentaries.

I've preordered my copy of the yet-to-be-made feature of *Thunderbirds,* with Andy Garcia and Sir Anthony Hopkins, so stay tuned!

Quick—think of as many great movies as you can that were based on comic books!

Yeah, me neither. In fact, if you pressed me, I might even prefer movies built around unfunny, one-note characters from *Saturday Night Live.* The world of comic books frightens me—all those dark, hideously deformed creatures committing odd, unspeakable acts. And those are just the people who read them. (Thank you! Thank you! Please, no. Really. Please. You're too kind. Sir, put the gun down!! No. Noooooooooo!!!)

But the fact is, I find the level of escapism in comic books unhealthy. Sure, I've been known to hole up in the basement for days playing *Doom* and reading *The Silmarillion* over and over, but that's just because I'm hiding from the evil elves who want to steal my third-level charm shield. If it gets to be too much, I'll know.

I did sneak out of my lair long enough to see two wonderful examples of the comic to movie translation: *Judge Dredd* and *Barb Wire.* They have much in common. Both are set in the future and feature maverick, outlaw heroes who triumph over evil—and both star really fleshy, stupid people.

Sylvester Stallone stars as Judge Dredd: judge, police officer, and executioner from *THE FUTURE*. He parades about in a shiny plastic ensemble the likes of which George Michael might place on one of his rock video funtime dress-up supermodels. It's not very flattering on Stallone. Perhaps that's why he lashes out so much in this movie, killing scuzzball after scuzzball in a hopeless attempt to mask his discomfiture at the sartorial indignities thrust upon him. Stallone should always wear loosefitting attire to mask his diminutive stature. This might mitigate his Short Man's Disease. Common to men of his height, it manifests itself in excessive weight lifting, jujitsu classes, and unseemly motorcycle riding (poodle-haired blond girls optional).

Quipping in this film is handled by Rob Schneider (the copier guy from *SNL*, a man who just won't go away). I was distracted by his presence, unable to shake the notion that he might at any time turn to his costar and say, "Judge Dredd. The Judge-a-lator. Judge-a-ludge-a-ding-dong. Making copies." It made me wish the puffy, androgynous "Pat" character had been his sidekick.

There are many digital effects in the film, and when you see them, you'll say, "There are many digital effects in this film." Lots of flying jet-skis go by, with many wonderful post-*Jetsons* sound effects—all of which will make you wish you had watched that rerun of *She's the Sheriff*.

If your life is going well and you have too much joy in your soul, try renting *Barb Wire,* and that should change things for you. Pamela Anderson Lee is Barb Wire, a freelance bounty hunter from *THE FUTURE*. I wasn't fond of Mrs. Lee's performance, though I should admit my prejudice in that I believe her to be a horrible, filthy bride of Satan. I rented the laserdisc version, which promises more "sexy footage" of Anderson Lee than the theatrical release. I assume they refer to the opening scene in which Mrs. Lee goes undercover as a stripper to return a kidnapped woman to her parents. For what seems like hours, the poor woman shakes her plastic endowments at the screen while being sprayed with several thousand gallons of some glycerin-water solution. It's chillingly unsexy, and you find yourself preoccupied with the physics of the situation, wondering exactly what polymer was used, thinking about viscosity and thermal breakdown. I would rather have seen more "sexy footage" of William Conrad in the laserdisc version of *Cannon*.

A running "joke" in the movie is that Ms. Wire does not like to be referred to as "Babe," and in one scene, a man who does just that gets speared in the forehead by one of her high heels, dying instantly. This gory, unfunny little moment could be interpreted as a feminist statement, but really only by the dwarfish, sebaceous little creatures who read comic books like *Barb Wire* and go weeks without seeing a real woman. And the women from their collections of superviolent Japanimation don't count.

When the film was over, I had the overwhelming urge to shower. A good, hot shower with mounds of antibacterial lather. The kind of shower that Meryl Streep got in *Silkwood*. So if you're game, buy a couple cakes of Lifebuoy and fire up the system!

DVD has made huge inroads with consumers, outselling goofy, multicolored underwear and even salt mills (for that "fresh-ground" salt taste). But retailers concede that the format won't be firmly entrenched until certain big-money classic movies are released, films like *North Dallas Forty* and Rick Springfield's *Hard to Hold.* Why certain studios are reluctant to release their best movies on a superior format is anybody's guess. It's most likely because they view the consumer with dismissive contempt and assume that every American is a lying, thieving pirate, holed up in his basement with mountains of dubbing equipment. What else could explain those accursed stickers on CDs and DVDs, the ones that gently suggest we "lift" off, only to have them split apart, leaving adhesive on our hands and the jewel boxes? We need expensive solvents to remove the glue, just to keep them from sticking to our pets. This dearth of classic movies leaves us with no alternative but to rent the current, big-budget action films that Hollywood insists we love (not watching anything is out of the question). Though *Jaws* is unavailable on DVD, there are 492 copies of *Mercury Rising* at my video store alone. They should simply have done with it and make every movie *Armageddon*.

Recently I gave in to the overwhelming pressure put on by the behemoth studios and rented *Event Horizon*, the action/sci-fi/horror epic starring Sam Neill and Laurence Fishburne. An event horizon is the area of a black hole from which no matter can escape. Or it is a crappy movie starring Sam Neill and Laurence Fishburne. I personally would accept either answer. In the film's reality, *Event Horizon* is the name of a ship designed by Sam Neill, who recently starred in a series of commercials hawking some sort of communications product wherein he peeps through a telephone jack at people doing the bunny hop around their office. It's disturbing to think that New Zealanders might be secretly looking at me while I work. It's hard enough to work with my dog talking to me all day long.

Anyway, the *Event Horizon* attempts time travel by creating a wormhole and flying through it. A wormhole, as I understand it, is an anomaly in space where . . . hell, I don't know. I think it has something to do with Worf or Hobbits or something. The *Event Horizon* gets lost in this wormhole and comes back seven years later, after blowing the mortgage payment on booze and cheap women, I guess. Neill plays the ship's designer, who leads a team of Space Soldiers, I think, to find out what happened to it. The movie, after whizzing its initial attempts at both action and sci-fi, tries out horror, and fails at this as well. Stealing an idea from countless *Star Trek* episodes, the ship begins recreating the inhabitants' worst fears and presenting them in short little playlets. The reason is unclear, but suffice it to say that the makeup designer got to smear lots of stuff with ooey, gooey blood! It's a moist movie, and sticky as well. There are lacerations and sores; eyeballs explode. It's as though the kid who wrote "Great Green Gobs of Greasy Grimy Gopher Guts" grew up and made his own movie.

You see, the ship went through the wormhole and ended up in hell. Not the "long line at RadioShack" kind of hell, or the "my date wants to see *The Waterboy*" type hell, but the actual dwelling place of Satan and his minions. Apparently Satan made some calls, found out where the ship was from and, rather thoughtfully, tried to return it to its owner. Only now the ship has the stink of evil all over it, which reduces its long-term resale value. Most of your evil vehicle owners will carefully detail them and may even put sawdust in the transmission so the buyer doesn't notice—so, caveat emptor! My problem with the whole concept, that being that the human race is a mere plaything to unspeakable supernatural evil, is that never once does anyone even think to mention God. You may say, "But the filmmaker's presenting a reality without God." And then you'd offer me a sandwich and get me a juice box. But then I'd reply, "Perhaps, but that's unfair in my book, because he's stolen the concept of hell from Judeo-Christian tradition but carelessly left out the central theme of that tradition." Then I'd accept your sandwich and ask if I might just have a glass of water, thank you. You might then say, "But then if someone introduced God into it, He, as the creator of everything, would simply squash the evil, and there'd be no movie." And I'd go, "Yeah, but . . . look, let's not fight. Let me just finish my sandwich and I'll get out of your hair. Suffice it to say, it's a stupid movie."

SPHERE

I frequently focus on the American family, specifically the American family and its application in crappy movies. Families are fine, as they go; it is now time, however, to shift our focus to something lasting and important—namely, DVDs. While we dawdle away the hours pondering commitment, morals, and relationships, precious titles are being shipped! Titles like *Highlander—The Final Dimension*, *Playboy's Celebrity Centerfolds*, *Playboy's Video Playmate Calendar*, *Playboy's Playmates Revisited*, and, of course, the digitally restored, 5.1 channel *Playboy's Babes of Baywatch*. It's really an embarrassment of riches.

The advantages of DVD, or Digital Versatile Disc (formerly Digital Video Disc, Digital Velocity Dog, and right before settling on its current name, Debbie's Velcro Davenport) are now well known. It has much higher resolution than VHS or laserdisc, and in many cases is better than the *actual* actor or scenery. The sound is a vast improvement, with DVD's ability to spread Skeet Ulrich's rich, sonorous voice over five discrete channels. Its quick random-access menus allow you easy access to your favorite monkey shenanigans in Matt LeBlanc's *Ed*. Many DVDs also contain extra material; for instance, the documentary *Burden of Dreams: The Making of Tommy Boy* might be found on your favorite David Spade movie.

I recently viewed a DVD that takes advantage of many of the format's strengths. *Sphere* (formerly titled *Ball* and *Round Thing*) is the Barry Levinson movie starring Dustin Hoffman, Sharon Stone, and Samuel L. Jackson that was out for seventy-eight minutes in theaters. *Sphere*'s lukewarm reception may be due in part to the tag line on the lobby card that reads, "Terror Can Fill Any Space." To my mind it sounds too much like an Earl Schieb commercial— *Terror can fill any space, for $49.95!*

Sphere, based on the Michael Crichton novel, is the story of a group of scientists investigating an alien spacecraft that has crashed deep beneath the ocean (they were probably on a manatee mutilating expedition). The craft has picked up a large golden medicine ball, the purpose of which eludes the brainy scientists, played by Hoffman, Stone, and Jackson. Not one of them arrives at the most likely solution: that it's simply a ball, probably used by some alien phys ed teacher to smash into the face of the smart but slightly corpulent kid who threatens his own masculinity.

As the less than brilliant scientists try to sort it out, people start dying, of course, until there are only a few of them left, etc., you know the drill. *Sphere* is the kind of movie that gives sci-fi in general its well-deserved reputation as the smelly, unemployed cousin of the entertainment family. Simple, half-baked moral messages are dressed up in wan intrigue, all of it shot on superdark sets so no one notices how bad it all is. Truly the central message of *Sphere* is the type that makes even the lesser stories on the original *Star Trek* seem profound.

The DVD features many extras, including an audio track with the voices of Dustin Hoffman and Samuel L. Jackson sharing their experiences in making the film. As talented as these two are, I'd frankly rather sit through Senator Orrin Hatch reading *The Uniform Commercial Code: Credit Union Reformer or Bane of Traditional Banking Laws*. I did manage to get through a few Samuel Jackson stories before I realized I had bullion cubes that needed sorting.

Once I had the beefs separated from the chickens and the vegetables on their own shelf, I took a crack at the documentary on the making of the special effects for the film. I'd frankly rather sit through a ten-hour tape of *The World's Greatest Aviation Weather Reports* as read by Garrick Utley. Fully half an hour or more is given over to a thin, pale man who stares at a computer screen all day making digital jellyfish. As necessary as digital jellyfish are, I personally haven't the patience for lengthy lucubrations on their makeup.

Despite its many flaws, *Sphere* illustrates the potential of the DVD software itself. I can personally foresee a time when we'll all be enjoying the audio track of Jason Alexander holding forth on the making of *Dunston Checks In,* or Dick Butkus's poignant notes on his part in *Mother, Jugs and Speed.* There are hundreds of us waiting for the restored version of *Welcome Home, Roxy Carmichael.*

Gene Roddenberry. Undoubtedly a prophet for our time. With unswerving dedication and a Promethean vision, he singlehandedly created the sci-fi genre and presaged the modern information age. Or maybe he was simply a perpetually stoned lech, whooping it up in his hot tub and cashing husky checks from an embarrassed Paramount Studios. It depends on who you ask.

The great man left clues, however, in his body of work, which includes the entire *Star Trek* franchise . . . and . . . that's about it. Unless you count the Popeye's Chicken franchise, which you can't, because he didn't create it. Neither can you credit him with writing *Black Like Me* because strong evidence exists that it was not he who wrote it. So it's *Star Trek* alone for which he will be judged, and not Clean Shower no-touch shower cleaner, because, well, he didn't invent it!

The unchallenged notion of his genius must crumble slightly, even for his staunchest admirers, when one takes a good, hard look at Pavel Chekov. Does any right-thinking person really want to live in a future in which at any moment a Russian-American with a bowl haircut might leap out at you and say "wessel" when he really meant "vessel"? And what if your name is Victor? Surely you'd punch him sharply and often after hearing, "Thanks, Wictor," and, "Whatever you're having, Wictor."

And what of Uhura and the giant piece of machined aluminum jutting out of her ear canal? I find present-day headphone engineering to be perfectly suited to my needs, and I happen to know many people who feel the same way. Cold pieces of drop-forged alloy rammed into the sides of our heads—this is no answer, and Roddenberry should have known that.

Further insights can be gained by watching any of the four hundred or so *Star Trek* movies. I made the mistake of viewing three in a row, without interruption. It induced a kind of dopey sci-fi trance—not unlike the effect of eating a whole picnic ham and reading Heinlein. To be fair, none of the movies, *Star Trek VI: The Undiscovered Country, Star Trek: Generations,* and *Star Trek: First Contact,* was that bad (okay, *Generations* was); perhaps I'm just not as delighted as others by countless references to the Argothiman Wars of Trimon 5 or the Wasnon Ale from the Caltritian Moons. And I admit I'm not scientifically adroit (my kindhearted physics teacher called me an "idiot"), but the technical references I find rather numbing. "Captain, the Valdothian tumomulators are reacting negatively to the pistofrian faldovs," says Worf, to which Picard might say, "Then notify the Redallions that we'll be needing Tarcuthian crystals for our bluthons, and pay them with Asprithian Tufars! Make it so!" And then he tugs down his polyester top and Worf makes it so and apparently I'm the only one who's not happy.

I'm also hopelessly confused by the other races—if I've got this right, there are Vulcans, Klingons, Romulans, and Remus. All currently have unsightly bumps on their skulls, yet in the original series they simply sported Rollie Fingers–like mustaches, correct? Some are good, and some are evil, yet all hate Kirk with a flaming passion that burns with the heat of a thousand suns. After seeing his death scene in *Generations,* I confess I share their passion.

On the subject of *Generations,* I need some help with the Nexus, too. From what I can gather, it's a large, dryer spark that sucks you up into it and makes you live eternally in the dullest part of your life. For me that would mean seeing *Generations* over and over again. Then perhaps someday I'll understand why Soran (Malcolm McDowell) dresses up like Sting and stands on top of a mountain waiting to get hit by the dryer spark. He could save time by simply drying a load of sweatshirts.

The most appealing thing about the *Star Trek* series is that many of the actors are as old as rocks. It really is refreshing to see a major motion picture that is completely free of Reese Witherspoons or young, hot guys named Skeet. There are people with lines on their faces, people with names like DeForest and George and Walt. Patrick Stewart's got some miles on him, and Nimoy!—he voted for McKinley, for crying out loud.

Star Trek is, after all, a pretty good space opera, but the idea that Roddenberry was a genius is on shaky ground, and when you throw in Wil Wheaton and Guinan and all the aliens with the latex appliqués glued to their heads, it all starts to seem uncomfortably similar to the things your first-year dorm-mate used to dream up when he was baked.

Come to think of it, I'm going to bake right now and try to make sense of the Nexus.

THE POSTMAN

I will once again focus on DVD, the break-through technology that is revolutionizing the way we watch idiotic action movies starring Bruce Willis. Pre-DVD-ian technology was "lossy" as far as delivering the correct amount of Willis's smirk, and it now seems nearly antediluvian the way we used to hear the sound of his flat, affected voice over just two analog channels. It is a far more engaging experience to watch Willis blow away some "@#$#@%^" using crisp, digital video and to hear "drop the @#$%^ gun, you @#$%^\!" over 5.1 channels of full-range sound.

If you currently lack DVD capability, you should know that it's relatively easy to acquire the equipment needed, provided you have a MILLION JILLION DOLLARS! Installation can be the tough part, and in my case I was told it was easier to remove my old house and install a newer, prewired home rather than go through the expense and hassle of rewiring the old one. I was also sold a superior eighteen-channel system, with thirteen of the speakers buried beneath the foundation (the foundation is made of silver, to avoid signal loss), providing antinoise to combat ambient "grunge" traveling through the soil. Of course, one also must have at least one hundred watts of power for every line of resolution on your TV, and it's always best to have more. Taking Trent's advice (Trent was my salesman at Big Top Audio), I also installed several outboard D/A converters on my couch, just as a precaution. You certainly don't have to follow my lead, but Trent says if you don't, "your system will totally suck" and "people will laugh at you."

Selecting the right speakers is key. Size isn't all that important, though a good rule of thumb is "pick a speaker just big enough to kill you if you tipped one on yourself, then buy one model number up." Position the speakers using lasers and mirrors, cover your room in thick, acoustical foam, and buy a subwoofer no smaller than a Hyundai Sonata.

Now you can calibrate it (a fortnight's process, involving many strange, odoriferous men with level meters) and you're set to start enjoying films like *The Postman,* directed by and starring Kevin Costner.

First of all, my condolences to anyone who inadvertently rents *The Postman* thinking it's the Italian film *Il Postino.* I can imagine their confusion over seeing Pablo Neruda riding through arid, postapocalyptic lands firing a black powder rifle at marauding bands of rag-draped looters.

The Postman sees Costner as yet another grizzled loner trying to make sense of a world without order. Thankfully, the film doesn't open with the aforementioned grizzled loner distilling and drinking his own urine, as in *Water-*

world. Though *you* may be driven to such extremes if you attempt to view the film in one sitting, without pausing to get up for a root beer. It's a very long film.

Costner plays a wandering actor who makes a few nickels by presenting scenes from Shakespeare with his ass. His donkey, that is, though it really doesn't make a difference. He is shanghaied into the army of the Evil Guy (whatever his name is), played by Will Patton. But he then escapes and begins bringing hope to the hopeless by delivering their letters, old J. Crew catalogues and coupons for free oil changes. Jammed into the plot is a weak romance between Costner and Some Woman (I don't remember her name, either) played by Olivia Williams. This was put into the plot so that Costner could have scenes of himself making love to a beautiful and talented British actress. Someday I hope to direct and star in a project I'm developing called *Mike Nelson Loves All the Lovely Ladies.* I'll star, if that's okay, and my costars will be Salma Hayek, Winona Ryder, Cameron Diaz, Olivia Williams, and Natalie Imbruglia for good measure.

The picture quality of *The Postman* is terrific, whether you care or not, and the sound is quite good, though the extras are fairly worthless. There's a small documentary on the making of the film, a cast list with bios, and my favorite, the recommendations. According to *The Postman's* recommendations, if you liked *The Postman*, you'll also like *Demolition Man* and *Sphere.* I don't doubt it. However, if you liked *The Postman*, you might also enjoy a nine-hour coach flight to Fargo, North Dakota, with a small child kicking your seat the entire way. At least these recommendations are fairly truthful. Normally, they're of little help: "If you enjoyed Sinbad's *First Kid,* you'll also enjoy Bergman's *Through a Glass Darkly.*"

Despite my reservations about *The Postman,* I'm fully enthusiastic about DVD and its possibilities. In fact, I'm meeting Trent tomorrow to upgrade to the molybdenum interconnects and the laser-deposited diamond speaker spikes.

PART FIVE

THE FIVE
FAMILIES
(Plus Two)

THE ARQUETTES

When we consider larger-than-life, mythical families like your Sheens and your Baldwins, we're talking about tall, proud men and women (well, men) who are unafraid to be weak in front of their families while starring in *Spawn* or *The Arrival,* or even TV movies with names like *A Bra Remains: The Kelly LeVieland Story.* Now let's look at a sprawling family whose roots in the entertainment industry are as deep as a mighty oak. (A *mighty* oak, mind you. Not one of those scrawny scrub oaks that you find growing in the sandy soil of northern Wisconsin. I might use one of those in an analogy for the Olsen twins or Hanson.) I speak of the Arquettes, who in Hollywood project the kind of stature mythologized by Barbara Stanwyck's family in *The Big Valley,* Lorne Greene's hearty brood on *Bonanza,* or perhaps Tom Bosley's mighty scion in *Happy Days.*

The taproot of the aforementioned oak (mighty, as you'll recall) is Cliff Arquette, aka Charley Weaver, whose career began in television and ended . . . in television. And always, whether on *The Tonight Show, The Roy Rogers &*

Dale Evans Show, or *Dragnet,* he was his beloved, rumpled character Charley Weaver. *Almost* always, that is, for on the show *Comin' Round the Mountain* he stretched outside himself and played Droopy Beagle, a role that taxed him greatly. He will be remembered by most for his long tenure on *The Hollywood Squares,* where his banter with Peter Marshall was never to be equaled, not even by the lightning-quick duo of Gene Rayburn and Shadoe Stevens.

Cliff's son Lewis Arquette strode, strides, and will strood (?) in his father's footsteps, starring in such films as *A Very Brady Christmas* (which I thought was only *fairly* Brady), *Rock 'n' Roll High School Forever, Chopper Chicks in Zombietown, Tango & Cash,* and *Rescue from Gilligan's Island.* The roots grow deeper still.

Chops learned from Bob Denver were clearly passed down to Lewis's son Alexis Arquette, who applied his training to his recent role in *The Wedding Singer,* starring Drew Barrymore and the Dark One himself, Adam Sandler. I saw *The Wedding Singer,* and I must confess I have no recollection of Alexis Arquette. This is not because his performance wasn't memorable; perhaps it was. I was just so traumatized at the sight of Adam Sandler as romantic lead, I lost my memory, my hearing, and my most recent meal. A kindly Gummi Bear salesman carried me from the theater and placed me in a cab, where with Herculean effort, I was able to sputter out my address. I arrived home to the arms of my wife, who nursed me to health by playing old episodes of *F Troop* until I was strong enough for solid food.

That misstep aside, the family grows stronger with the

performances of Alexis's brother Richmond, who has appeared in *Se7en* (should you ever meet the person who came up with that cutesy title, please don't hesitate to slap them), *The Pickle,* and *Gridlock'd,* which, according to my source, had great success in Hungary, where it was known as *Az Utolosó Belövés.* As long as he sticks to films destined to be dubbed into Hungarian, I see nothing but good things for Richmond, or Riçkmònst, as he'll soon be known.

Brother David has had recent success in the satanically bloody, tragically self-referential *Scream* series playing opposite the bony Courteney Cox. He also appeared in *Airheads,* which starred the late Chris Farley, Steve Buscemi, and, agghhhhh, *Adam Sandler*!! I'm getting light-headed. . . .

David's sister Patricia has had a great measure of success in such films as *True Romance, Flirting with Disaster, Lost Highway, Beyond Rangoon,* and *Ed Wood,* in which she brilliantly portrayed the bald, hulking Swedish wrestler Tor Johnson. Her greatest challenge now is her relationship with the balding, hulking former Coppola, Nicolas Cage.

Arguably the first Arquette to make a huge impression was sister Rosanna. Unfortunately she made the impression on Toto lead singer Steve Lukather, who immediately penned the treacly megahit "Rosanna." If there's one thing I've learned in life, it's to *not* make an impression, favorable or otherwise, on any member of the band Toto. One treacherous day I struck up a friendly conversation with the big-haired guy from Air Supply—*and it nearly cost me my life!* Rosanna, it should be noted, was once married to former Elton John producer James Newton Howard, now a composer who has scored nearly sixty films, among them *Waterworld*, *The Devil's Advocate*, and *Glengarry Glen Ross*, in which Al Pacino played the role originated by Joe Mantegna on Broadway. Joe Mantegna, you may recall, starred in *Airheads* with . . . Adam Sandler!

THE BALDWINS

Tolstoy would have us believe that every happy family is happy in the same way. I for one don't buy that. It's impossible to imagine a family happy having learned their father will be released from his ten-year imprisonment in a gulag sharing the identical emotion with the family that has just won a meal for six at Pearson's Big Steer Restaurant. Tolstoy's an idiot for even suggesting it. Does he really expect us to believe that the happiness shared by the Marx Brothers, having just pummeled Margaret Dumont with body blows, is the same as that shared by the Howard brothers, Moe, Curly, and Shemp, having just extracted their dear friend Larry's head from a tight mine shaft? Tolstoy's starting to look like more and more of a jackass with each fresh example.

The count's muddleheaded bromide angers me because I have such reverence for the family (the Wayans being a notable exception). Humans in general, I think, share that reverence and are fascinated by the conquests and tragedies of public families: the Rockefellers with their scandal, money, and philanthropy; the Kennedys as America's royalty; the Smith brothers and the vicissitudes of the cough drop market.

In a world where the stability of the family is being eroded by longer work weeks, phat pants, rice steamers, and Hot Pockets, it's nice to see a stabilizing force like the Baldwin family out there reminding us what's important. Alec, Daniel, William, and Stephen are the public face of the clan Baldwin, but their collective body of work hints at stern, loving parents and perhaps a few other siblings. Orville and Wilbur Baldwin, or Zeppo Baldwin, perhaps. We can only speculate (unless we wanted to actually look it up on the Internet, but that would be really sad).

Alec, of course, is the figurehead of the family—the oldest and, in many ways, the least likely to run about naked in a cocaine haze. His movie career is surely the most respectable, including as it does roles in such diverse films as *Working Girl*, *The Shadow*, *Glengarry Glen Ross*, and *Forever, Lulu*. *Lulu* starred Debbie Harry of Blondie fame, and filthy-mouthed midget Dr. Ruth Westheimer. Alec's film career has mostly overshadowed his costar Westheimer, though rumor has it she is being considered for the title role in *Tattoo You: The Herve Villechaize Story*.

However, no amount of starring in *The Juror* or *The Shadow*, or marrying Kim Basinger, is going to wipe out the memory of Alec's having starred on TV's *Knots Landing*. But he can at least medicate the pain with manly film roles in *Miami Blues*, *The Hunt for Red October*, and *The Edge*, in which he tangles with a large, slobbering brute, the freshly knighted Sir Anthony Hopkins. I understand there is also a bear in the film.

Brother Daniel Baldwin will in all probability never tangle with an honorary knight on-screen, unless he gets in a fistfight with the notoriously snippy Sir Elton John and it makes the ten o'clock news. (I can only guess that the match would be all Baldwin, with perhaps a few decent kicks by Elton connecting now and again—unless Bernie Taupin threw his hat in the ring as well. Then it's anybody's fight.) Daniel doesn't have many screen credits to his name; most people know him from the television show *Homicide*, which I believe is about homicide. It will be interesting to see how the family rallies around Daniel after his recent drug problem. I hope they offer help and support and not just a role in *Bio-Dome II*.

William is one of the younger Baldwins, kind of an ur-Baldwin, who has starred in such films as *Sliver, Backdraft,* and *Fair Game*, with Cindy Crawford, herself star of such films as, well, *Fair Game*, with William Baldwin. *Sliver*, as you no doubt recall, starred Sharon Stone in unpleasantly close contact with both Baldwin and Tom Berenger. I never saw the film, though I understand it's a psychological thriller about two men trying to remove a small splinter of wood from the skin of a beautiful young woman's hand with tweezers.

Stephen is the youngest and dumbest member of the family, working as he has with the beneath-contempt Pauly Shore in *Bio-Dome,* and allowing himself to be shackled to Laurence Fishburne in the wan *Defiant Ones* simulacrum *Fled.* Many consider him the Gen-X Baldwin, which works out on my conversion chart to be the equivalent of Sporty Spice. (By law, all comparisons must be made in Spice Units, or the writer is subject to heavy fines and lashings of their latest CD.)

Whatever hardships they endure, they're certain to go through it together. As a family. A family with agents. And lawyers. And PR firms. But certainly secure in the knowledge that, if one of them calls, the other's personal assistant will get back to them as soon as they can.

We can only hope our own families are that strong.

THE CULKINS

Though we all live under the umbrella of protection offered by one of the thirty-seven greatest countries in the world, there is a shadowy danger lurking just around the corner of our local Starbucks, just past the Cineplex Odeon, over by the PetSmart, not far from Boston Market, near the Wal-Mart, and even by the Honey Baked Ham store next to the karate school. It is the very real danger that Macaulay Culkin could have any one of us killed! Yes, if we are to be honest with ourselves, it must be admitted that the popular little moppet could call a hit on us in broad daylight, and the Justice Department would simply look the other way. Culkin has achieved the kind of power that usually resides in the realm of fiction, and much like a Bond villain, Culkin could melt the ice cap or detach the state of Florida and we as a nation could only watch helplessly, most of us secretly delighted that we don't have to put up with Florida anymore.

But amongst even his staunchest supporters, a blasphemous whisper circulates: Is Mac losing his chokehold on the American public? Will children stop after a mere 374 viewings of *Richie Rich?* Would the dance belt he donned in 1994's *Nutcracker* fetch even a C-note on eBay?

Yes, there are ever more wily Daniel Sterns and Joe Pescis lurking around the Dark Tower, the Barad-dûr-like fortress that Culkin and his father Sauron have constructed. The *Pagemaster–Getting Even with Dad* combination was to have made him Emperor of the World, yet that failure is said to have made deserters of his dark army. Even his loyal Orc lieutenants, John Hughes and Chris Columbus, have been seen hiding out in the shadows of Khazâd-dûm. (For more extended Tolkienian analogies of child actors, pick up my book *Saruman in Tap Shoes: The Films of Shirley Temple.*)

An examination of Culkin's oeuvre might yield clues as to the current state of his empire, or it might simply yield mild nausea. Culkin started his film career in 1988 with *Rocket Gibraltar,* a film I've never seen, nor have any of the several friends that I polled during a recent game of street hockey. Perhaps that was his first mistake—signing on for a film that would be unknown even to random street hockey players. Next came 1989's *See You in the Morning.* Ditto. One guy, a friend of a friend wearing a Packers stocking cap, at first said he'd heard of it, but under pressure realized he was mistaking it for *The Morning After,* starring Jane Fonda and Jeff Bridges. Again, a huge misstep for Culkin, being in a film whose title sounds vaguely like another film title.

In 1989, Culkin and his unnaturally red lips hit it big with John Hughes's *Uncle Buck,* starring the late John Candy. *Uncle Buck* utilizes the threadbare formula of having a large unorthodox person, animal, or professional wrestler enter the family dynamic, teaching them, and himself/itself how to love . . . again. It's been done successfully in films such as *Mr. Nanny*, with Hulk Hogan; *First Kid*, with Sinbad; *Beethoven*, with a St. Bernard; and *A Long Day's Journey Into Night* with Sir Ralph Richardson.

Uncle Buck was the first of the John Hughes–Culkin collaborations that would rule the early 1990s, a time when people guzzled clear beer and wondered if they were nasty enough to call Janet "Miss" Jackson.

Culkin made a short stopover in Adrian Lyne's *Jacob's Ladder*, playing a tab of LSD, I think, before making his magnum opus, *Home Alone*. In it, Culkin played the pigmentless scion of John Heard and Catherine O'Hara who gets left behind when the rest of the family vacations in Paris. Though this was technically negligence, I support the parents fully. Round-trip tickets to Europe are spendy, and almost certainly the French would not have reacted well to the treacly little upstart. Dry existentialism, body odor, and clove cigarettes are incompatible with pink little tykes in Gap Kids chinos.

Home Alone has made roughly $398 trillion dollars to date, with most of that going to Culkin's salary for *Home Alone 2*.

Culkin's rough spell began with 1993's *The Good Son*, in which he played a future serial killer, and *The Pagemaster*, a lighthearted animated biography of Johannes Gutenberg. He followed that up with *Getting Even with Dad*, a film that opened in 2,200 theaters and was seen by 11 people. The theater owners' take is half, meaning *G.E.W.D.* grossed exactly $38.50.

After that disappointment, Culkin needed to strike back

big. The answer: Slap on some tights and gad about in a tepid production of *The Nutcracker,* a show so oft-produced that on any given night in December more than three quarters of the world is performing it somewhere. There are decent productions of it at many local RadioShacks.

So what's next for Culkin? Well, clearly, he snaps. His dad can't be safe. And after that . . . it's one of us.

DILLON BROTHERS

Everyone remembers where they were when they first heard Dylan. Certainly most first-time listeners were baked to the gills and would be hard pressed to remember what dorm they lived in, but with a bit of coaching or perhaps some deep hypnosis they could recreate a credible memory of their initial exposure to the towering folkie. Personally I couldn't be bothered with him, as there are only so many hours in the day and *Big Country* was consuming the vast majority of them. (*Big Country* and Old Style beer, that is, because their special method of *krausening* seemed to help my studies.)

On a different note, it's harder to imagine anyone dredging up a memory of the first time they saw Matt Dillon, unless that memory were piggybacked on a memory of, say, being hit by a bus, or marrying Tiny Tim, or some such life-changing event. Fewer, still, are the significant memories surrounding brother Kevin Dillon. Taking it even further, maybe three people remember the first time they saw Melinda Dillon; and not a single human being, his closest friends included, remember seeing Dylan McDermott for the first time.

Allow me to refresh your memory as it pertains to the brothers Dillon, Matt and Kevin.

Kevin is the younger brother, remembered by many for his role as Bunny in *Platoon,* the last Oliver Stone film that anyone could stand. Dillon was terribly effective in that film, in large part because he looked so much like the kid on the playground who instilled in others the unshakable belief that, if crossed, he would kill you. (If you *are* that person, thank you for taking the time to read my book, and please know how much I understand how badly the world has hurt you as it has hurt me so many, many times. It's us against them, my friend!)

Kevin shocked everyone by going electric in Oliver Stone's *The Doors*. He was tolerable as John Densmore, but the entire production left one with the impression that someone had spilled bong water all over the film stock, and they all thought it was funny. It probably doesn't help that I've always loathed Morrison. My personal list of the most despised people runs roughly like this:

1. Satan (and his minions)*
2. Hitler
3. Jim Morrison
4. Pol Pot
5. Steve Miller

---

*The inventor of the leaf blower actually tops the list, but I have yet to find out his/her name.

Even if you are a fan of Jim Morrison's poetry (and if you are, may I say, thank you for taking the time to read my book, and please know how much I understand how badly the world has hurt you as it has hurt me so many, many times. It's us against them, my friend!), you can't deny that his voice is very much like any given dad's voice singing clumsily from the shower as he soaps his beefy arms. Just stop for a moment and imagine Morrison's ham-fisted baritone shouting out his idiotic free verse "Break on through to the other side," and now imagine your own father in his tiled stall mindlessly singing the same verse. See? They're indistinguishable!

Kevin Dillon's complicity with *The Doors* is, in my book, a tacit admission that he's a huge Jim Morrison fan, allowing me to put him on my list of world's most despised people. (I've lost several dear friends in the same manner, an unfortunate situation that could have easily been avoided had they simply not brought up the Lizard King, as all right-thinking people should take care not to do.)

Kevin's brother, Matt, has never openly confessed his love of Morrison, allowing me to speak tentatively thereof.

Matt came to the world's attention in Francis Ford Coppola's *The Outsiders* and *Rumble Fish,* both from 1983. I remember seeing these films when they came out, but in all honesty had only half an eye on them as I was watching *Big Country* videos with the majority of my concentration.

These roles led to his breakout performance in *The Flamingo Kid,* opposite Richard Crenna, a man so perpetually dadlike as to be perfectly suited to play Morrison in *The Doors II: The Other Side.* Dillon was decent in *Flamingo*

Kid and has done some good work since, in *To Die For, Singles,* and *Drugstore Cowboy,* but he, along with brother Kevin, always excels playing guys who normally ask you what you want on your sandwich at Subway. It's a legitimate niche, one that used to be handled by your Michael J. Pollards or your Timothy Bottomses. Now, however, Pollard and Bottoms are *actually* the guys making your sandwich at Subway. (But I kid Pollard and Bottoms. I'm mostly likely going to pull one of them as shift manager some day.)

Kevin and Matt are talented enough to avoid such a fate. If not, just ask them to go light on the oil, and no jalapeños.

THE SHEEN/ ESTEVEZ

"Family" is a controversial word in this age of computers, virtual pets, and the new, longer-lasting Fiberglas roof shingles, but that's exactly what I want to talk about now: family. (Not *Family*, the TV series. For information on that, pick up my book *When Eight Is Not Enough—A Critical Analysis of the Lance Kerwin/Kristy McNichol Legacy*.) The word "family" incites controversy precisely because it is hard to define. To me family means Tuffskin jeans, big bags of economy-sized puffed rice, and silent meals of Tuna Noodle Hot Dish. I suspect it means the same to roughly 90 percent of all people in the Midwest, but we can't be sure of that. There are those, I'm certain, who grew up in a household where both parents were professional jugglers, and for them family means endless loops of *The Sabre Dance*, scorn, humiliation, and a house littered with tiny beanbags. I don't share a common experience with those from juggling families—nor with those from *any* of the circus arts, for that matter.

Therefore, as a place to start, I suggest we all agree to define family using one word—Sheen. Well, Sheen/

163

Estevez. Well, specifically, Martin Sheen, Charlie Sheen, Joe Estevez, and Emilio Estevez. So, nine words. There are probably some moms and sisters in there somewhere, but since none of them have starred in films like *The Arrival, Men at Work,* and *Spawn,* I think we can ignore their influence and move on.

We have Martin Sheen, the father; Charlie Sheen and Emilio Estevez, the sons, and, of course, Joe Estevez, the uncle. Their struggles and triumphs are all there on the big screen and the ever-growing rental market in such films as *St. Elmo's Fire* (parenthetically, Elmo is a fine if cloying *Sesame Street* character, but is he really worthy of canonization?), *Beverly Hills Brats,* and *Young Guns 2.*

I recently rented *Spawn* ("that's your own damn fault," I hear you saying, and you're absolutely right), starring Martin Sheen, aka Ramon Estevez. Now, *Spawn* is not the worst movie ever made. Wait . . . yes it is. It is the worst movie ever made. It's hard to discipline your children for being in *D3: The Mighty Ducks* when you yourself are acting next to a foul-mouthed, gas-expelling John Leguizamo in a fat suit. To be fair to Martin, there was a time when he was in better movies, like *Apocalypse Now, Badlands,* and *Captain Nuke and the Bomber Boys.*

It's hard to know what influence Martin has had on his brother Joe's career, though his filmography does yield several clues. Joe, a larger, scarier version of Martin, has starred in such vehicles as *Soultaker, Blood on the Badge,* and *Beach Babes from Beyond,* with *Don* Swayze, *Joey* Travolta, *Jacqueline* Stallone, and, well, Burt Ward. In many cases it's not an altogether bad idea to buy an off-brand of aspirin or cornflakes, but if you're reduced to purchasing off-brand quasiporn movies starring the impostor fragrance equivalents of Patrick Swayze, John Travolta, and Sylvester Stallone, it's time to trim other things from your budget and do the upgrade. Patrick Swayze, John Travolta, and Sylvester Stallone are *already* off-brands of actual actors. You don't want to take a further step down, or you'll end up in Adam Sandler territory.

In Emilio Estevez's oeuvre, one can hear the echo of the elder Sheen's words. Words like, "Grab for the long green, kid, even if it means being in a crappy Disney quickie." And, "*Freejack*? Hell, yes! Are you nuts?" Emilio wrote and directed the film *Men at Work*, in which he costarred with his brother, Charlie. *Men at Work* is the story of two down-on-their-luck garbage men who shoot their neighbor with a pellet gun. If it doesn't sound all that compelling, please remember it was written by Emilio Estevez. I saw it with a friend on its opening night, because we wanted to see the worst movie we possibly could. That was 1990, and *Spawn* was many years away.

The family must have worried for Charlie, starting as he did with such relatively respectable roles in *Wall Street* and *Platoon*. But Charlie soon did the family proud, signing up for *Navy SEALS*, *The Rookie*, and *The Chase*, costarring Kristy Swanson, of *Mannequin 2: On the Move* fame! (Incidentally, *On the Move* costarred Terry Kiser, who costarred with Andrew McCarthy in *Weekend at Bernie's*. Andrew McCarthy costarred with Emilio Estevez in *St. Elmo's Fire*. What a wonderful world!)

Charlie added to the family legend by becoming a member of the frequent buyers club at Heidi Fleiss's place. It became well known that he purchased the ladies' services to act as though they were cheerleaders *on the night before a big game!* That's the kind of detail that only the son of an actor can provide.

That unpleasant detail aside, it's important to reflect on just how many families have been brought together by *their* family watching such films as *Touch and Die* and *Roswell: The UFO Cover-up.*

None, I'm sure. But thank you for taking the time to reflect with me.

THE PENN BROTHERS

As I look back on the families whose work and lives I have examined as a critic of megacheese, I can think of none whose story is as bold and thrilling as the clan I turn my attention to now. As maverick as the Wright brothers, as tough and devoted as the fighting Sullivans, as pouty as the Judds—such is the Penn family. Chris, Sean, and Michael Penn are a kind of gritty Osmonds, their talent extending as it does to such varied media.

The Penn family was founded in 1681 when father William Penn was granted the land of what was then West Jersey in a settlement with Charles II. He envisioned a place where his sons could settle and, without fear of persecution, star in movies such as *Footloose, We're No Angels,* and *The Game.* He sought for his sons the freedom to record songs with lines such as "what if I was Romeo in black jeans," for at the time such grammatical failings might be corrected at the pillory. One might even be forced to wear a scarlet T.P.H.T.G., meaning, "This Person Has Terrible Grammar." It was George Fox himself who bade his countrymen to abolish this draconian punishment, and through his tireless efforts it was eventually shortened to G.N.I., a more humane representation of "Grammar Needs Improvement."

The Penn family has unswervingly carried out their father's unique vision, or so recent viewings of both *Footloose* and *The Game* have convinced me. *Footloose* (1984) starred Michael Penn, Lori Singer, Dianne Wiest, John Lithgow, and, of course, Kevin Bacon, whose father, Sir Francis Bacon, lord chancellor to James I, envisioned a world in which painstaking scientific method would be utilized in the making of such movies as *He Said, She Said*.

In *Footloose,* Chris Penn did what he does best: play a gape-mouthed idiot. It was Chris who tried to convince the young firebrand Bacon it was unwise that "everybody cut, everybody cut. Everybody cut, everybody cut. Everybody cut, everybody cut. Everybody cut footloose." Chris was effective in this movie in large part because his appearance and mien are the antithesis of those who like to cut footloose. I remarked same to some acquaintances of mine at a gathering where all of us were cutting footloose, and everyone agreed.

Bacon plays an outsider in a decidedly foot-tight town whose citizenry think so little of themselves that they allow John Lithgow to boss them around. By doing stupid dances and improbable gymnastics in a dusty barn, Bacon is able to convince them that the wisest course is indeed to cut footloose. When the movie came out, the country agreed, and the broomstick-thin Kenny Loggins led us all in endless choruses as we happily kicked off our Sunday shoes. It was a giddy and wonderful time.

While Chris was at the center of this phenomenon, brother Sean was busy helping wife Madonna develop her frightening, conical breast missiles (both fashionable and practical, the breastplate allowed Madonna to post amazingly low drag coefficients in test after test at a Nevada wind tunnel), as well as starring in *Shanghai Surprise.* Sean had already made a name for himself in *Fast Times at Ridgemont High,* a monstrously successful film in which he played a gape-mouthed idiot. While Sean has turned in a number of great performances in films such as *Racing with the Moon* and *Dead Man Walking,* as well as directing *The Crossing Guard,* he should be led off in stocks for his complicity in making *The Game* with Michael Douglas.

The Game was directed by the pointlessly bleak David Fincher, known mostly for directing lousy music videos and ruining whatever momentum the *Alien* series had gained by directing the third. He also directed *Se7en,* a movie so pornographically gruesome that he should be imprisoned and have his eyelids forced open while Madonna's *True Blue* video plays in an endless loop.

The Game stays true to his cynically dark and childishly formulaic vision. In it, Michael Douglas plays a cold, reptilian millionaire whose black-sheep brother, played by Penn, buys him an enigmatic gift. It is a game, of some sort. Had it just been Scattergories, they could have played a friendly round and we all could have gone home ninety minutes sooner, our minds blissfully uncluttered by images left over from old Duran Duran videos. As it is, though, the game turns out to be a murderous trap, etc., etc. There's a "twist" at the end, but it's the kind of twist that might have promise in a Huey Lewis video, not a motion picture for thinking adults.

As far as brother Michael is concerned, well, we haven't heard much from him since his breakthrough album, featuring the hit "No Myth," was a runaway success.

Though I know it isn't my place, I timidly suggest that he consider "cutting footloose" as a possible career move.

Raising a family has become an extraordinarily difficult task, especially in today's increasingly complex world. Children point and laugh at you when you suggest that their hair could use "a little vegetal and perhaps some fixative." They turn their noses up at the victuals you offer, even refusing such sweets as pasteboard and starched milk, which is doubly frustrating, dry goods being as dear as they are these days. And look out if they happen to get ahold of your motorcar, for it's off to some groggery or alehouse to bend an elbow with the topers and eyeball the chippies.

Tough as it is, my family succeeded roundly, using a combination of liberally applied soup-based casseroles and a method of discipline not unlike that used by Huck Finn's father, only without the tenderness. For other families different methods are more successful. Ed McMahon and Tony Randall, who both have newborns, use a method whereby the father is certain to be 138 years old when the child reaches middle-school age. By then, the father has mellowed a bit from the tempestuous "one hundreds" of his youth. With Michael Jackson's growing family, you can be sure that at every stage of their development, a chilling broomstick-thin Pan-being will be cooing "The doggone girl is mine" into their tiny ears.

And for the Wayans family, to whom we turn our attention now, the method for success is simply *sheer volume.* There are, quite simply, *several hundred* Wayans. Like a good-sized college, there is a low citizen-to-Wayans ratio in this country, probably in the neighborhood of fifteen to one. In fact, in the United States of America alone a woman has a Wayans *every three and a half minutes*! If you started now, it would take you forty-seven years to view the movie output of a single Wayans, with no bathroom breaks.

At last count the performing Wayans were Cara Mia, Damien, Damon, Damon, Jr., Keenen Ivory, Kim, Marlon, Michael, Nadia, and Shawn.

I only scraped the surface of their massive and daunting output, so I suggest we put together a well-funded, multinational information-gathering team to report back to a centralized staff who can begin to gather data and suggest strategies for viewing the mountains of entertainment that the Wayans put out every several hours.

I muscled my way through *I'm Gonna Git You Sucka,* the 1988 parody of blaxploitation films, as well as *A Low Down Dirty Shame* and *The Last Boy Scout,* with Damon Wayans and Bruce Willis.

Though I confess I didn't find *I'm Gonna Git You Sucka* funny, it must also be noted that the film was in all probability not meant for me, a timid white man who grew up in a small outer-ring suburb of Chicago. I have not seen *Foxy Brown, Superfly,* or *Shaft,* so many of the jokes are lost on me. Although I have seen *The Other Side of the Mountain* several times, if that helps.

I feel more qualified to comment on *A Low Down Dirty Shame* because a knowledge of Ron O'Neal films is not a prerequisite. *Shame* was written and directed by Keenen Ivory Wayans, who cast himself in the lead, most likely for tax reasons. It's a fairly trite private eye story with a twist, the twist being that it's really stupid. Jada Pinkett contributes most of the stupid by playing Peaches, Shame's secretary. Pinkett's scenes do go on longer than you can imagine, stretching far out into the event horizon. Though I don't understand the physics involved, I know that you can watch her scenes in a moving car and come back home just in time to see yourself leaving.

The Last Boy Scout is a stupid movie *and* a sign of the end times, all rolled into one superviolent package. Though Willis, a specialist at stomach-churning violence, turns in another half-whispered, sub–Eric Roberts performance, it is neither he nor the uninspired Damon Wayans who must shoulder the blame. Its screenwriter was Shane Black, the author of *Lethal Weapon, Last Action Hero,* and *The Long Kiss Goodnight.* Black was paid a record amount for his screenplay, which consisted of several gun battles separated by misogynistic obscenities strung together in a manner that would make a drill instructor blush. Dozens of stable boys working tirelessly for weeks couldn't muster the filth of a single Shane Black line.

And so, after three Wayans movies, I retire. And until

we assemble our multinational committee, someone's got to keep watching! Perhaps prisoners can do it, or college students who need extra cash for their groggeries and gin mills. Get watching, you rakehells and hoydens, or it's a mulcting for you all!

PART SIX

CHIK FLIX

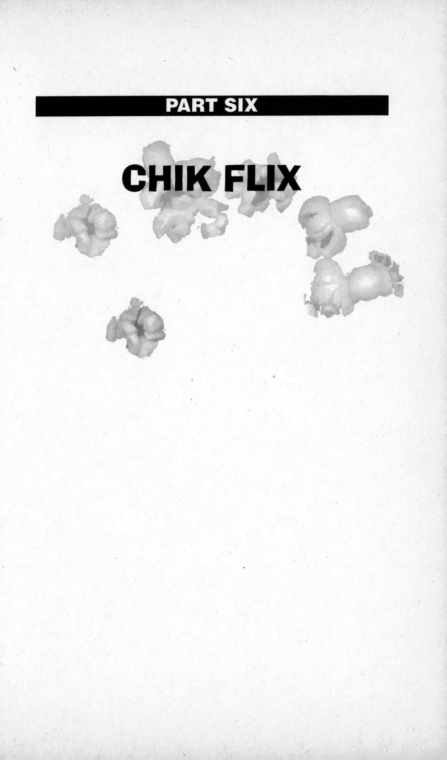

MY BEST FRIEND'S WEDDING

What are the elements that make up a good chick flick? (Forgive the inclusion of this possibly offensive term. I feel its universality and musical rhyming quality more than make up for any offense it might cause.) It must have a woman or women in it, I daresay. It should depict human emotions at some point. General themes of romance should be touched on or, if possible, hammered on. Clothes should be shown, of course. It must be free of any scenes containing rocket launchers, and at no time should the lead actors punch each other repeatedly in the face or kick one another's groin for any length of time. Any scenes of exploding helicopters would certainly disqualify it.

Other than that, it should star either Julia Roberts or Meg Ryan.

My Best Friend's Wedding meets all the criteria, as far as I can tell. It's exceedingly woman-y, containing as it does a woman in its lead role. It seems to depict emotion, though I admit I'm trusting my wife's assessment there. It was explosion-free, had crying, and, as a bonus, portrayed a gay man dishing dirt.

Its heightened femininity made it no small difficulty to rent without risking some erosion of my reputation as an extremely, almost monstrously heterosexual man. I couldn't ask my wife to rent it for me, for fear it would raise all sorts of questions in her mind. Renting it through the mail would leave a paper trail a mile long. Hiring a discreet third party to rent it for me only gives rise to more complications. That left only one possible option: to dress in full drag and rent it myself, incognito.

Makeup was applied, panty hose pulled on, bra stuffed and snapped, wig bobby-pinned securely in place, and soon I was ready to go rent *My Best Friend's Wedding* head held high, my manhood intact. It was exciting and somehow deliriously freeing to be striding up and down the aisles, able to rent *Little Women* or *Fried Green Tomatoes* without fear. As I gamboled about, prancing here and there in my shimmering little dress, I found myself reclaiming parts of my manhood I didn't even know I had lost. I capered home, made a mug of chamomile, pulled the blinds, and watched *My Best Friend's Wedding* from start to finish.

Julia Roberts, who exploded on the scene in *Pretty Woman,* the delightful tale of a ragged hooker hired by her predatory john to be his escort for the week, takes the role of Julianne, a New York City restaurant critic whose best friend, Michael (Dermot Mulroney), is about to get married. She and Michael were lovers for one brief, tempestuous month; now, as friends, instead of enjoying bouts of volcanically passionate lovemaking, they swap pasta recipes and lend each other Toni Morrison novels. I'm sure Michael is just thrilled with this arrangement. Julianne confesses to her gay pal George that she is still in love with Michael and intends to stop the marriage and win him back. This is a phenomenon I was warned about shortly after announcing my engagement—that women I had once dated would appear, seemingly out of nowhere, professing their love and begging me not to get married. Luckily for me, none of these women ever materialized. Frankly, I'd expected a little better turnout. Well, they probably just got hung up somewhere.

Julianne meets her competition, Kimmy (Cameron Diaz), and immediately launches a campaign of savage mental cruelty. She lays traps and plots, scheming like Richard III, or Mr. Drysdale, even, to get Kimmy and Michael apart. But it's not easily done, as theirs is a love based on the shared knowledge that they're both good looking. At one point, she shanghais George into her evil plotting, and he reluctantly poses as her fiancé. It's a gag worthy of *Three's Company,* missing only Norman Fell as an impotent caretaker.

When all her plots fail one by one, Julianne does the only sensible thing: She puts on a tiny sweater that lets her tummy show, and thrusts out her chest. She also puts herself in situations in which she's required to jog short distances. Her breasts do the best they can, but in the end, Kimmy marries Michael and they fly off to be good looking together.

When the movie was over, I felt let down. My dress was bunching, and my makeup was beginning to run. It almost seemed odd that I was in a dress at all. What do women see in these films, I wondered? Julia Roberts is as cute as a button, but she didn't have to do anything difficult like jump from a motorcycle onto a moving car and then beat up a dozen or so terrorists and throw them off the car to their death.

Perhaps they're saving that for *My Best Friend's Wedding II: Payback Time.*

For many, the transition from model to actor is a smooth and natural move—think of Lauren Hutton's towering performance in Burt Reynolds's masterpiece *Gator.* It worked for her, and continues to work for so many models, precisely because they spend so much of their time acting. They act as though they're not chain-smoking, rock-stupid Ex-Lax addicts, day in and day out. But if I could be serious for a moment, it can't be easy to have to explore the entire range of human emotions, from pouty to sullen, while being spurred on by a guy named Radu or Falco or Cicci, with phrases like, "sexy like a tiger" or, "let me feel your heat."

In trying to be supportive of models' desire for range-expanding roles in film, I rented both *Her Alibi,* with that Eastern Bloc looker Paulina Porizkova, and *Fair Game,* starring the bemoled beauty Cindy Crawford.

Her Alibi is a comedy, I think. Let me check the box. Yeah, it's listed as a comedy. It was made in 1989 as a starring vehicle for Paulina, who was well known for being kind of attractive, and for being married to Ric Ocasek, a man whose head, I feel, compares quite favorably with Lyle Lovett's. Her alibi is Tom Selleck, who plays a really bad mystery writer who hasn't had a successful book in a while, and so begins stalking Paulina, hoping somehow that will help. He lies to get her off on a murder charge and then moves her into his house hoping to write a novel dumb enough to make a million jillion dollars. In the process, shenanigans ensue, with lots of hijinks and tom-foolery. Paulina is being followed by scalawags, rakehells, and ne'er-do-wells, and so there's plenty of waggery and goings-on, knavery and gamboling, beer and skittles, and I don't know what.

Sad to say, Tom Selleck actually has a hard time hold-ing his own against the neophyte Porizkova. But then, Sel-leck would have a hard time holding his own against a shoehorn. Don't get me wrong, he seems likable enough, but it's clear that he should just shave his mustache and peddle exercise gear on QVC.

In the end, it's an amiable movie, no worse than a lot of things. Like getting a paper cut with thermal fax paper. Or listening to a discussion of the various merits of different kinds of growth funds in which to invest the holdings of your 401K. Paulina fares well enough, though I notice she's not stealing roles from Helena Bonham Carter.

The makers of *Fair Game* seemed to be hedging their bet with Cindy Crawford. They only brought out one of the lesser Baldwin brothers, an ur-Baldwin, if you will, I don't remember which one. Gummo Baldwin, I think. This sad bastard gives it the college try, but he's dragging a safe in Crawford. She was okay as hostess of MTV's *House of Style,* saying things like, "First, our story on summer. Then, we'll talk to people who like to have fun," while wearing a terry wrap, but she's over her head uttering lines like, "Let's get out of here!"

That doesn't mean that *Fair Game* isn't worth watching. On the contrary I can honestly say it's the most delightfully bad movie I've seen since *Road House,* the *Fanny and Alexander* of bad movies.

In *F. G.,* as I hope it will soon be known, Crawford plays a high-powered divorce attorney, and the demi-Baldwin plays a cop who must protect her from an impossibly ruthless and well-equipped mob of ex-KGB agents. Such is their power that when Cindy orders a pizza with her credit card, the devilishly clever commies show up at the safe house where she's hidden, *within minutes!* Uh-huh. The same people who can go through eight quarts of vodka in the time it takes to wait in line for a small lump of withered cabbage are tapped into every pizza delivery computer in the entire country. If that's true, the guys at Pizza Paradise could sell me out in a heartbeat.

The saddest moment in the film is the obligatory sex scene, that which finds the pasty Baldwin rubbing his hairy body all over the obviously detached Crawford as wan David Sanbornian music wafts through the *Silk Stalkings*–style scene. It's about as sexy as a concrete piling. The screen doesn't so much as sizzle as parboil. You'll want to shower.

That moment aside, *F.G.* delivers more laughs than the oeuvre of Adam Sandler <u>and</u> *Down Periscope* combined. I strongly recommend you rent it, but not to the exclusion of *Henry V* or *Look Back in Anger*. Let's not get crazy.

As far as models go—I think they should stick to rubbing hemorrhoid cream under their eyes and spray-gluing bikinis to their butts. Of course I think that of everyone.

THE MIRROR HAS TWO FACES

Apparently *The Mirror Has Two Faces*. One is the mirror's formal, Sunday-go-to-meeting face, the other a knocking-around-the-house face. Sometimes it's nice to just throw some sweats on your face and not care at all how it looks.

The Mirror Has Two Faces, directed by and starring Barbra Streisand, is the story of Barbra Streisand and how utterly fabulous she looks. There are ripples of plot to be seen here and there, but mostly it's about Barbra Streisand and how inconceivably beautiful and well preserved she is. Jeff Bridges is in the film somewhere, but he is set decoration, a mere sconce lamp, there only to illuminate the transcendental magnificence of Barbra's pulchritude. At least, that's how Barbra had it planned. Personally I thought George Segal, as Jeff Bridges's pal, looked even more radiant than she. He seems to keep himself in good shape, and his skin care regimen is obviously top-notch.

The film opens by introducing us to Gregory (Bridges), a handsome mathematics professor who finds sex a mere roadblock on the way to a meaningful relationship. He even shuns no-strings-attached sex with leggy math groupie Elle Macpherson. This fiction makes suspension of disbelief a Herculean task. That there are math groupies, I mean. Despite mountains of empirical evidence, it's taken me many years to accept the fact that '80s hair-band Night Ranger had groupies. I can't make the leap to mathematicians, not without hard data and plenty of counseling.

Gregory announces his warped and shameful (I think) no-sex policy in a personal ad in the paper. The respondent's looks are not even an issue, as sex is out of the question. For all Greg cares, the love of his life could be a fifty-seven-year-old over-the-road trucker named Barry. (Women, please don't allow yourself to think that because Gregory has evolved beyond the need for sex, there are men like him in the real world. It is purest fiction. Put it out of your mind.)

He ends up on a date with Rose (Streisand), arranged secretly by her beautiful older sister, Claire (Mimi Rogers). I'll restate that last part: her beautiful *older* sister, played by Mimi Rogers. Now, Barbra Streisand was born at some time during the Taft administration and is at least eighty-eight years older than Mimi Rogers. There's no shame in being old (unless you're one of those guys with those mandatory Old Guy Houndstooth Hats), but you tax your audience when you play more than a century younger than your actual age.

Gregory and Rose begin dating and, before long, he asks for her hand in marriage—with the proviso that they keep their marriage sexless. ("A needless redundancy," I might say, if I were Alan King or Mrs. Roper.) The arrangement works pretty well. Gregory is happy, Rose relatively so. She even tries teaching the poor, sheltered dope about baseball, explaining batting averages while Jim Leyritz is at the plate. Though she does a fine job elucidating baseball statistics, she doesn't even make an attempt to explain Jim Leyritz's deliberately bizarre, almost hostile stance. He looks like Nureyev winding up to club a harp seal.

Anyway, after pressure from Rose, Gregory relents and agrees to give sex a try. It is disastrous—no better than the sex college football players can manage after drinking a case and half of St. Pauli Girl. She decides she can't live under the current arrangement, so they agree to split for a while, easily agreeing that he can take all the books on set theory. While he's away on a lecture tour, Barbra begins a remarkable metamorphosis in which she loses weight, gets a makeover, and buys a cheap dress. When Gregory returns he's stunned to see that she's six ounces lighter, has ugly poodle hair, and is, well, wearing a cheap dress. With her newfound confidence, she's able to tell Gregory that she's moved beyond him, that she needs to feel attractive and vivacious, and that she needs to devote more time shampooing with botanicals and tea tree oils. After spending several miserable weeks in which he can barely concentrate on Gauss's gripping *Disquisitiones Arithmeticae*, Gregory decides he can't live without her.

One of the frustrating things about the film is the tonal dissonance between the script and Streisand's appearance. She's supposed to be very unattractive and yet she's unwilling to look even slightly rumpled. She was a fine-looking woman, fifty-five years old when the film was made. She should act her age—start getting used to the taste of Ensure and Feen-a-mint; get a start at buying the first of many crisp blazers and neat slacks; begin asking for discounts on bruised produce. This tarting about, playing roles that should go to Ally Sheedy, has got to stop.

The Mirror Has Two Faces is a fascinating glimpse into the febrile mind of a megalomaniacal lunatic—and it has a peppy theme song! Streisand finds it unthinkable to appear in front of a camera lens that hasn't been covered with a number-ten can of petroleum jelly. Her fingernails have been crafted from solid blocks of pure bulletproof polycarbonate. She is bathed in a heavenly light at all times, giving one the unsettling feeling that she's the target of an insecure alien abduction. I fear that she's stepped completely off the beam, that soon she'll begin bathing in the blood of virgins or that she'll marry James Brolin, the surest path to utter madness.

Unless she gets some serious clinical help, we're bound to see her as the title role in the next *Madeline* movie.

Parenting is probably the most difficult task in the world. If you don't believe me, just ask Sally Forth, a woman who manages to juggle family *and* career—and does it all with out losing her brittle sense of humor, or that inky black stack of solidified hair that sits atop her deformed head. That she lives in a house with that spooky, sarcastic kid and doesn't go completely bat-shit is testimony to how strong a woman she is, no matter how stiff and unnatural her body may look.

But Sally's just a cartoon strip. For examples of real courageous mothers, we have to turn our attention to the movies. Blondie, for one. There was a woman whose husband was at a subhuman intelligence level—box turtles found him insufferably obtuse—yet she stuck by him, loved him completely, even as he crammed his idiot face full of monstrously large sandwiches or physically assaulted their mailman. He was no help as a father, so Blondie was left to raise their children, Baby Dumpling and Cookie, virtually on her own. Undaunted by the fact that they were both small food items, Blondie raised them to be actual humans (except Baby Dumpling, who took after his father).

In the '90s, parenting becomes even more complicated, especially in the Chris Columbus film *Stepmom,* with Julia Roberts and Susan Sarandon. Columbus, who like his namesake believes that he is actually in India, is a protégé of John Hughes and has directed *Mrs. Doubtfire, Home Alone, Home Alone 2: Lost in New York,* and *Home Alone 3: Lost in a Foster Home.*

Roberts plays Isabel, a shallow, conniving homewrecker who tries to insert herself into the lives of a weak-willed father and his two unsuspecting children (I admit, my own biases may be getting in my way here). Ed Harris plays the father, Luke Harrison. Luke is in the Business, business where he makes over $89,000,000 a year with his company GeneriCo. Unfortunately his job leaves him little time to deal with his life, and when he lets his guard down, Julia Roberts steps in, becoming his girlfriend before he has time to object. Luke has a vague memory of children somewhere in the back of his mind, and sure enough, it turns out there are two of them and they're both his with his ex-wife, Jackie (Sarandon).

The film is essentially a chronicle of a nasty custody battle—set to syrupy music. And though I'd certainly like to believe that any parent would do everything in her power to fight for the best interest of the children, it's tough to accept in the case of these kids. Why can't Hollywood pick children? It was Richie on *The Dick Van Dyke Show* who set the bad precedent. He was a horrible, shrill child who attempted to use his cuteness like a cudgel, beating the audience mercilessly with his adorableness.

Luke's boy, Ben (Liam Aiken), is a just slightly more ani-mate Muppet, or maybe an updated Mason Reese, the kid from the Underwood deviled ham ad. Luke's girl, Anna (Jena Malone), is sour and mean, like a very young Denny's waitress.

The drama takes place as they go about their normal life: launching radio-controlled boats, horseback riding, putting on school plays with $300,000 budgets. Does Columbus have any idea what real people do? (Not that the movies should always have to depict real people. If that were true, how would you account for Jim Carrey?) People don't horseback ride; they go to Target and buy socks. I'm not suggesting that he make a movie showing people doing the mundane; I'm suggesting that he *thought* he had made a movie showing people doing the mundane. He's out of touch, probably because he's so rich from the *Home Alone* series and the money he scammed off Queen Isabella of Spain.

Because the plot is going nowhere, they give the Saran-don character cancer, and she responds by angrily sweep-ing everything off the countertop surfaces, which as we all know is what you do when you're in a rock video, not a Chris Columbus film. To ease the pain of cancer she begins smoking dope, which works well but has the unfor-tunate side effect of making you think that Kansas was really a pretty good group. The worst thing for her is knowing that Roberts's character will raise her children when she's gone. The only thing worse would be knowing that *Eric* Roberts is going to be raising your children when you're gone.

Roughly 45 percent of the film is comprised of characters grabbing hairbrushes and lip-synching to comfortable old Motown songs. Musically the film wants you to know it won't hurt you. It plays gentle, thorough music. Familiar songs—songs you already know, and know well. There are no sharp edges on the soundtrack; they've all been covered in a thick layer of protective foam. This is music that smothers you gently.

I think the music's duty is to distract your attention away from the fact that the film is really, really long. It's a Möbius strip of repeated scenes, and though it seems to go on for hundreds of thousands of years, it's actually longer. I believe this is the first film whose duration represents an *actual infinity*. I'm not talking about a *potential infinity* (e.g., whole numbers) that can be represented on paper only, but an *actually infinite period of time*. This means, of course, that I'm still watching *Stepmom*, which I am, even though I finished watching it some time ago.

I approached a point where I thought an ending might be coming (it was illusory) wherein Sarandon has the children come and say good-bye to her as she lies dying on the bed. She explains her death to her son by using the analogy of a caterpillar changing into a butterfly. She leaves out the part where she squirts the sticky liquid from her spinarettes, covering her body in a hard casing in preparation for her pupal stage.

On the DVD there's a bonus featurette included. The interesting thing about it is that watching it immediately after watching the film adds no time to the whole experience—because the length of the movie is an actual infinity! If you add one to infinity, you still have infinity. Even if you watch *Stepmom* an infinite number of times, you'll still have watched it no longer than the person who watched it only once.

Now if they could make a Muppet film even half that length, I'd be able to keep my kids busy long enough to get my lawn mowed.

THE BRIDGES OF MADISON COUNTY

When it was announced that Clint Eastwood was tapped to direct the film version of the phenomenally popular book *The Bridges of Madison County,* many were concerned that Clint's two-fisted style was less than appropriate for the delicate subject matter. After all, the story heartbreakingly chronicles four days in the life of an Iowa housewife who longs for more excitement than even Iowa can provide. Clint is more comfortable with material involving greasy guys robbing liquor stores or motorcycle-riding orangutans. Still, I don't think anyone could have predicted how many open gun battles Clint would sneak into the damn thing! Francesca, the lonely housewife, fires clip after clip at her stoic husband, who escapes into the cornfield in his souped-up Charger. Francesca gives chase in a stolen police car, blasting his back window out with several shots from her illegally stashed shotgun. Later, when rugged photographer Robert Kincaid (Clint) makes a move to kiss the vulnerable Francesca, she produces the Glock she had taped to her back and gets off three quick rounds before Kincaid overturns the kitchen table and returns fire with his (what else?) .44 magnum.

But I have fun with Clint's image. There was, of course, almost no violence in *The Bridges of Madison County*—none if you discount the scene where Francesca shoots out Kincaid's tire and his car crashes spectacularly through one of the titular covered bridges and plunges into the icy water below.

Again, I kid. Clint's version actually opens with a prologue wherein Francesca's children discover a diary detailing an affair she had had many years before. I don't know if this particular framing device was part of the book, because I didn't read it. I didn't read it because I'm a man. No man read the book. The author, Robert James Waller, didn't read the book, and certainly neither did Clint. That should not be taken as a judgment on the quality of the book, certainly. It's almost always unfair to judge any work without reading it, with the exception of the novelization of *The Santa Clause*. It's just that every man knew instinctively that *The Bridges of Madison County* involved romance and woman stuff. Sure, men may even have been curious to know why the book was so popular with women, but there's no reason to read when you've got Al Michaels.

We see into Francesca's past as she sends her family off to the Illinois State Fair to enter their prize steer and, even though it's the 1960s, catch the Oak Ridge Boys at the grandstand. Francesca, in her loneliness, makes the first of more than six hundred pitchers of lemonade that she will produce during the course of the film. As she lounges, free from any fear of contracting scurvy, a beat-up truck rumbles down the dirt road to her farm. A man gets out; a rugged man, a man with a head like a large rawhide chew. Like most people who end up in Iowa, he's lost, so she agrees to take him to the charming covered bridge, where they will begin their torrid Iowagian affair.

The leather-headed man introduces himself as Robert Kincaid, a photographer for *National Geographic,* who's been assigned to shoot pictures of the bridges of Madison County. She introduces herself and explains that her husband is from Iowa and so she needs to get laid. I'll allow that the movie was subtler than that, but that's the general drift.

Things go slowly. They have dinner together—good, hearty food, freshly killed. Kincaid's pickup lines are clumsy but effective. Africa is his favorite place on earth because "...there's no imposed morality," just "the cohabitation of man and beast, beast and man." He tells her he's "a citizen of the world," that he's fed up with America because "there's too many lines being drawn. 'This is mine—he or she is mine.' I think I just embrace the mystery." Now, really, Clint—put the bong down and come up with a real line. The guy's so dreamy and vague, you expect him to pick up a guitar and start singing "Suite: Judy Blue Eyes."

She falls for his line of crap and accompanies him on his photo shoot the next day, completely forgetting about her family, the whole lot of them suffering heat, pig offal, and the sounds of Willie Nelson. His day of work done (he took maybe four pictures; if I were her, I would've checked to see if he even had film in the camera), Grandpa Clint takes a hot shower at her house. When he's done, she follows after and we hear her in voice-over: "I realized he had been here just a few moments before. I was lying where the water had run down his body and I found that incredibly erotic." I find it incredibly disgusting. Clint's used bathwater as an aphrodisiac? He was wearing a fairly thick flannel shirt, crawling around in the tall weeds—the guy's a magnet for deer ticks and black flies. All manner of skin oil, dirt, dander, and body hair could be mixed up in his soupy gray runoff. Painfully hot water and a half a can of Bon Ami first, *then* hop in after Clint. You'll feel even more erotic knowing his sebaceous discharges aren't sluicing around in there with you.

Freshly bathed, they head off to the hippest jazz club in all of 1965 Iowa. There are hepcats in bib overalls getting down while the players blow bebop and modal jazz. Keep in mind this is Iowa; 1965 Iowa. Must have been in Oskaloosa or Creston. I guess Clint, a huge jazz fan, just couldn't resist. I'm just glad he's not a big fan of Joe Jackson or Cutting Crew.

Their dalliances must end, of course, for when the last stall has been hosed down, her family will return. It's best not to greet your loved ones while locked in coitus with a gristly photographer—unless you're trying to cut all ties with your family, that is. Then it can be a fairly effective way to avoid those awkward Thanksgiving get-togethers. Clint offers Francesca the chance to come with him, to live out of, or possibly even in, a suitcase for the rest of her life. Though it pains her, she declines, knowing she must stay with Richard, if only to save him the humiliation. Besides, Richard's a good man, and although he can't offer her the exotic mysteries of Africa, he does know an oat mixture that will provide 20 percent higher yield while maintaining the animal's resistance to disease. Clint, heartbroken, leaves her to go off and nab his magazine yet another picture of a cute kid saluting the American flag. Richard returns and, unaware of her indiscretion, goes about his job of being laconic. He's the apocryphal Midwestern farmer who loved his wife so much, he almost told her.

If you can get over the fact that it depicts infidelity in languorous detail, then there are some charming moments in *Bridges*. Meryl Streep is always good, and it's fun to see if Clint's elaborate hair structure will hold. Clint's getting older and letting his hair grow fairly long, necessitating that he sweep the imposing gray mass back and freeze it into shape with rigid fixatives. It makes him look a little like a frightened, elderly clown. A *handsome* frightened elderly clown. A clown who could still clean my clock without even copping a bead.

So, if you enjoy slow films featuring geriatric circus performers making love, *The Bridges of Madison County* is for you.

WHAT DREAMS MAY COME

Those seeking satisfying answers to the ultimate questions will discover in time what every seeker throughout the whole of human existence has discovered: Nothing is "knowable." Scant solace is available, and despair looms. We side with Peter De Vries when he writes: "We are nothing but a string of gut on a stick of bone riding this piece of astral soot for one piteous splinter of eternity." Belinda Carlisle's assertion that "Ooo, heaven is a place on earth" rings hollow, and most of us look for deeper answers. Prince insists that in this world "things are much harder than the afterlife" and that our only hope is to "go crazy." Prince has gone crazy, and it's served him well, but for most of us this isn't an option: If we go crazy, someone will have to cover our shift at the drugstore, and that's not fair to him. To David Byrne, heaven is a bar, "a place where nothing, nothing ever happens." Keep in mind, however, that David Byrne is a man who has a great deal of trouble purchasing a suit jacket of the proper size, and should not be trusted in eschatological matters.

Different religions seek to answer these questions—some even attempt to provide hope and comfort—but affiliation with many of them brings with it occasional requests for fruit salad or a pound cake. Most of us seek spiritual answers that don't require us to bake.

Director Vincent Ward's film *What Dreams May Come* is a complete theology of the afterlife, starring Annabella Sciorra and *Mork & Mindy's* Robin Williams. It tells the story of Chris Nielsen (Williams) and his wife, Annie (Sciorra), and how their lives are shattered when Chris begins donning a red jumpsuit and communicating with an alien known as "Orson." Their marriage dissolves, and Chris buries his head in the sand, repeating sadly, "Nanoo, nanoo."

Not true, of course. The film opens with a scene from the past, as Chris and Annie meet on a lake in Switzerland and fall immediately in love. Even the sight of Chris's Elton John–type hair can't cool the flames of Annie's passion. She marries him, hair and all, and they lead a perfect, diamond-commercialesque life together until tragedy strikes. Chris's puffy hair deflates. Soon after, both their children die in an automobile accident. I was laughing at the film's maudlin style until that point. Then I had to get serious because of the subject matter; though I have to admit it felt as though the director knew his audience might be snickering and so he threw that in there to shut everyone up. It felt like getting yelled at by your teacher for laughing in class.

It's four years later, and Chris is trying to pull his wife out of her depression. He does this by putting on silver boots and flying around in an egg-shaped spacecraft. It doesn't help. Chris is killed in an automobile accident when a driver going 130 mph hits a small ramp left in the road and lands on top of him. It's unclear why the driver didn't see Chris, but this being the '90s it can be assumed he was talking on the phone, eating a Bacon Lover's DeLuxe, faxing a proposal to the Dubuque branch, putting in a Livingston Taylor CD, and taking a sip of Sumatra Mandeling Dark Roast. Chris's death throws off Annie's whole week, and she plunges even further into depression. She attempts to cheer herself up by listening to Morrissey music, but it makes matters worse.

Chris, now quite dead, is able to see Annie and even talk to her, though his voice is vague and difficult to understand—about the quality of sound you get over the Internet. He is being led on his spiritual journey through the afterlife by a nude, blurry man whom he calls "Doc." Doc pleads with him to let go of his life and follow him into the hereafter, and he also asks him to do that killer penis routine he did on *Comic Relief III*. Chris makes the decision to follow Doc (actually his mentor, Albert, in life) and soon finds himself in an enchanting world where he slips around a lot because everything is made of oil-based paints. "This is the world you're creating in your own mind," Doc informs him. God apparently ripped the idea of heaven off that one *Star Trek* episode where Kirk chases his old rival Finnegan and Bones falls in love with a woman who wears a dunce cap. Doc/Albert cuts a fake wall out of Chris's made-up world and shows him a world beyond it, the real heaven, a place where plump cherubs constantly strafe the locals and people walk around looking rather detached and sad.

When Doc/Albert can't make it to show him around one day, a kindly Asian flight attendant named Leona helps out. She walks him around, vaguely explaining the workings of heaven, which frankly appears to be rather shoddily run. Just when Chris is getting used to Leona's particular brand of evasion, she reveals herself to be Chris's daughter, Marie. Why did she purposely deceive him into thinking she was not his daughter but rather an Asian flight attendant named Leona, you ask? Aha! . . . well, it's never really explained. I can't help you there.

Back on earth, Annie, overwhelmed by hopelessness and grief, kills herself. Again, I was just getting up a good head of steam giggling over the film's greeting-card visual style and confusing plot and then, a suicide. Now I can't laugh anymore or I'll get in trouble. Albert/Doc gives Chris the news and then informs him that he's actually his son, Ian, and offers some weak excuse as to why he's been going around heaven lying his ass off. Albert/Doc/Ian has more bad news: Annie is in hell. She'll be joining the red-wigged Broadway Annie who is spending an eternity there as punishment for singing "Tomorrow."

Chris hires The Tracker (Max von Sydow) to lead him to his wife so he can talk her into coming to heaven (no one is sentenced to hell in Ward's theology—it's a kind of voluntary lockup). The Tracker leads them through a nightmarish landscape reminiscent of Bosch (Jake Bosch, my barber. Okay barber, *really* bad painter). He finds his wife and dutifully brings her to heaven, where they live happily among the overfed seraphim—until they decide to be reincarnated, an option available to the inhabitants of heaven, though it's not clearly stated in the brochure.

What Dreams May Come really looks like it took a lot of work to make, which is too bad, because it's not very good. Its theology is totally incomprehensible. Rules are established and then abolished just as quickly, even though Albert/Doc/Ian states, "There are no rules here." God exists, but doesn't seem to care, and He takes no pains to spruce heaven up at all. The devil doesn't exist, and God doesn't punish anyone, so it remains a mystery as to who made hell and why. People can be reincarnated, or not, it's really up to them. As to souls, there is no mention of them, though it's stated that people are made up of their thoughts. It's the theology of a couple of guys doing bong hits.

To quote Bryan Adams, "I'm findin' it hard to believe this is heaven."

NORA EPHRON/
MEG RYAN

Many people these days decry the lack of romance in modern society. To them, I say, "Well, maybe it's you who aren't romantic. Did ya ever think of that? Huh?" I admit, it's a childish thing to say to someone leveling a reasonable social criticism, but I feel as though I'm holding up my end of the whole romance thing. As an example, for Valentine's Day I bought my wife a v.90 56k modem to take advantage of our digital phone line, *and* I even bookmarked a Web site where she can order herself a card online! Tears filled her eyes, and she ran from the room—I knew I had hit pay dirt. Are swooningly romantic gestures such as mine really all that rare? I think not, if reports of brisk digital modem sales are to be trusted.

For men out there, you don't need to be Cyrano to keep romance and chivalry alive. Next time you are with a lady and you approach a door, wave your hand out in front of you to trip the infrared signal on the automatic opener so it doesn't have to be the motion of *her* knee or *her* arm that trips it. It's a small thing, but women appreciate it.

And women, here's a suggestion to rekindle romance: Leave a trail of notes, starting at the front door, leading through the living room, another in the family room, till of course it ends at the refrigerator, where a four-pack of Guinness in the can, the ones with the nitrogen inserts, sits waiting next to a six-pack of Harp in the bottle. His heart will melt.

Perhaps the most visible sign of romance on the modern landscape is the trilogy of films starring Meg Ryan and written by Nora Ephron. *When Harry Met Sally, Sleepless in Seattle,* and *You've Got Mail* make the most tender, lush ballads of the immortal Nat King Cole look like a big pile of crap (my analogies need work, I admit).

When Harry Met Sally is the nonfiction account of the historic meeting of Harry Carey, Jr., and stripper Sally Rand, and the tempestuous sexual relationship that followed.

Or, more accurately, it chronicles the lives and loves of Harry Burns and Sally Albright, two opposites who meet on a cross-country trip. On that trip, Harry (Billy Crystal) tells Sally (Meg Ryan) that men and women can never truly be friends without the issue of sex mucking everything up. This is most certainly untrue—in my premarriage days every woman I encountered made it quite clear, either through violent yelling or raucous laughter, that a sexual relationship with me was quite out of the question. We were then free to be platonic friends, provided I made no attempt to write to, call, or contact the lass in any way.

Many viewers will smile in recognition as Harry and Sally stroll about the beautiful cityscape, getting in fights and faking orgasms. It reminds me very much of my own youthful relationships, minus all the malt liquor and constant Billy Squier music.

For 1993's *Sleepless in Seattle,* writer Nora Ephron also took the reins as director and made an unapologetically romantic and cloying film. And it's not very subtle. Watching it is like being stabbed repeatedly with a Twinkie, or being beaten with a bag of doilies. It's like drowning in a pool of rose water or being forced to drink molten Hummel figurines. It's kind of like having pictures of cute kittens tattooed on the backs of your eyelids, or getting buried in an avalanche of lemon chiffon. You get the idea.

The tag line for the film was, "What if someone you never met, someone you never saw, someone you never knew, was the only someone for you?" Well, then we're all hosed, because we've never met, seen, or known this magical person and we're all stuck with the horrid beasts we've got now. What are we supposed to do about it, anyway? Keep up a run of unprecedented infidelity until we find that one someone? And what if she lives in the Australian outback or deep in the rain forest? I don't have the resources to start an affair with someone in Malaysia, and I'm certain my wife wouldn't chip in to finance it, especially if she was seeking her own "only someone."

Well, *Sleepless in Seattle* shows us how it might go. It tells the story of widower Sam Baldwin and his son, Jonah, who picks up from Chicago and move to Seattle to get a fresh start and to get away from all those Chicago-ites who can't stop telling you how great Chicago is. Plus, in Seattle there's a coffee shop every other door, not just one on every block, and they can get discounts on Spin Doctors CDs.

Sam just can't seem to get over the death of his wife, and living in the same town as the Frugal Gourmet hasn't lifted his spirits at all. Jonah attempts to get help for him by calling a radio psychologist who cajoles him into putting his father on the line. Sam does, and after telling his story he becomes the latest heartthrob to all the women who stay up late listening to pop psychologists on AM radio. (I myself have attempted to attract females by getting on the radio and pretending I'm a sensitive widower with a small child, but I can only get through on *The Stretch and Toddmonster Sports-a-thon Show.* Consequently my only interest is from guys who claim to love me but only want to know if I think the Vikings are going to be vulnerable to the run again this year.)

One interested listener is Annie Reed (Meg Ryan), a reporter from Baltimore who is in a committed relationship with Walter, a very decent man who treats her well. Walter will, of course, be shot out of the saddle at some point, and the audience will need some reason to accept this; therefore, Walter has allergies, the poor idiot. (This is a feature common to all Nora Ephron movies: the main characters are already in committed, sexual relationships, and are usually living with partners or fiancés. I personally find it hard to sympathize with a main character, even one as cutesy-pie as Meg Ryan, when I know she's just rolled out of the sack with Bill Pullman or Greg Kinnear and is inevitably going to end up with Tom Hanks.) Annie can't get Sam off her mind and is soon even misusing her resources as a reporter to fly out to Seattle and stalk him. It's charming when Meg Ryan stalks a man. Less so when, say, a large, whiskery man with a gun collection and a shriveled hand stalks Meg Ryan.

Sam, unaware of his stalker, has started a relationship with Claire (Dana Ivey), a perfectly serviceable woman, who, because this is a Nora Ephron movie, must get dumped, and soon, because there's not much of the movie left. She does, and the only roadblock that remains in the way of Sam and Annie's magical adulterous relationship is the sad-sack Walter and the inability of his immunoglobulins to distinguish between animal dander and real parasitic invaders. Over a lovely dinner, Annie confesses to Walter her love for a man she's only heard over the radio and seen through her high-powered nightscope. Walter, instead of doing the manly thing by crying and punching a car, behaves like a gentleman and lets her go gracefully. What the hell is that all about? It's his job to haunt her life for several months afterward. He's supposed to fall apart so that she feels guilty. If he had any guts, he'd show up drunk at weddings that they were supposed to go to together. Any real man would send her tapes of Cure songs they both liked, or call her once a month at closing time and ask her drunkenly, "Are you happy? I zjust w'nna make zsure you're happy." I suppose Ephron was showing men how women would *like* them to behave when they get dumped. Well, I'm afraid as long as there is malt liquor, women will have to expect messy breakups.

The film ends happily when Jonah, the annoying son, runs away and hops a plane to New York. One can assume it wasn't a Northwest flight, because he got decent service and his meal choice was available when they got to him. Sam gives chase, and they all end up together, Sam and Annie falling immediately in love; presumably, until she hears an even more pathetic wretch on some late-night call-in show.

Sadly, it ends before we can see whether Walter can pull it together and maybe yell something obscene at Sam and Annie's wedding.

You've Got Mail (1998) is allegedly based on an old movie and a play, but was, in reality, based on a .wav file attachment in the America Online software. That .wav file doesn't hold up as a full-length movie. It should have been expanded to a .jpeg file and shown to test audiences before making the leap to film.

Once again, Meg Ryan stars as the puppy-cute lead, and this time she's taking no prisoners. She's backing up the adorable truck and unloading pallet after pallet of precious; box after box of winsome; hundreds of tons of darling. Tom Hanks counters with full clips of Everyman charm.

Kathleen Kelly (Ryan) runs a bookstore called The Shop Around the Corner, which sells nothing but adorable books. Anything not deemed irresistible is returned to the distributor. She is in a committed, live-in relationship with Frank, but is cheating on him with some creepy stranger in one of those dirty America Online "chat rooms." (I wish they'd stop forcing the linear comparisons to real life. It's not a "room." People are not "chatting." People "chat" in "rooms" at parties where they are "next" to "each other" and where "drinks" are "served.") The creepy stranger turns out to be Joe Fox III (Hanks), who is soon to open a gigantic Fox Books mega-store right around the corner from Kathleen's shop. Joe is living with Patricia, but since she's mildly annoying and is played by Parker Posey, she's easily expendable.

We viewers mustn't be tempted to let the fantasy of the movie creep into our own lives. Meg Ryan is not "chatting" with us on AOL. No one who looks like Meg Ryan is chatting with us. No one named Meg is chatting with us. The only Meg, Stephanie, or Veronica who chats with anyone out there is a large man with abundant back hair and unbelievably potent body odor. Guys, if there is any void in your relationship that you think is being filled on-line, keep in mind the person filling it has a beer gut and is named Dan. And remember you're filling a void in his life. Ladies, especially those of you who resemble Meg Ryan . . . well, you don't need any advice, because you don't chat on-line.

This shadowy world of late-night chatting works out perfectly for Joe and Kathleen, however. Their live-in lovers are dumped, and they're free to frolic about in idyllic Manhattan. This fantasy Manhattan is enthused about by director Nora Ephron in a special section of the DVD edition that gives you a tour of *Mail*'s locations. She gushes about perfectly ordinary-looking hot dog stands and coffee shops as being near as you can come to heaven. Why is it Manhattanites insist that you agree how unapproachably spectacular their city is? We don't do that here in Minneapolis, mostly because we have no self-esteem, and, well, there's not that much to brag about, unless you count the pretty tasty grilled cheese at Embers. Sure, Manhattan is an amazing place, if for no other reason than its ready availability of sushi at 2:00 A.M. But it's loud and very crowded. There are lots of those business guys, who I grant you have every right to cram together in small spaces and do whatever business it is they do. But as they walk down the street in great, unsmiling packs, they radiate waves of sadness, and if you're not ready for them, they can intimidate you—make you think you should be doing something more important than just trying to find sushi. Plus, at any time, a hot blast of urine-scented air can hit you. If you're a certain kind of person, it might be of your own doing, but for the vast majority of walkers, it's unwelcome. And it happens a lot. Nora Ephron doesn't mention that.

I'm fully aware that's it's never a good idea to end a column on the subject of romance by talking about hot blasts of urine-scented air, so I'll simply sum up by suggesting that these films, though romantic, are but suggestions of the real romance available to anyone who is young at heart. For instance, in just a moment I'll be turning up the temperature setting on our water heater so that my wife doesn't have to use the loud, long "pot scrubber" cycle of our dishwasher.

Men—get out those toolboxes and make some romance!

PART SEVEN

THE LEGENDS

BRANDO

Marlon Brando: A legend, to be sure. Perhaps even as talented as the other legend named after the majestic game fish—Marlin Perkins. It's even safe to say that in hand-to-hand combat, Brando's weight advantage would most assuredly put him on top (provided Jim Fowler and his accursed helicopter-deployed snare nets stayed out of the fracas).

But, alas, this argument will have to rage forever unresolved, as Mr. Perkins was unable to avoid the powerful hind legs of death itself.

What does this have to do with the film career of Marlon Brando? Sadly, nothing. But the never-to-be-seen cage match of Perkins-Brando remains one of the most provocative intellectual playgrounds left to a generation bereft of such imaginary pugilistic pairings. Only the Rip Taylor–Rip Torn showdown is as challenging, and some hold hope that it may actually happen, though it remains doubtful.

But, Brando! The colossally overrated superstar has recently contributed to what I believe is one of the worst films in 157 years. I speak, of course, of *The Island of Dr. Moreau.*

I would give you a synopsis of the film, but to do so would be as difficult for me, and as helpful for you, as giving you a synopsis of the fever dream I had as a child when I saw cats jumping over my head in great fans. Or the time I drove long distance, quite tired, and hallucinated Tolkienesque giants striding out onto the median of I-94.

I did discern that it starred Val Kilmer. Kilmer, you'll recall, is the hard-to-work-with actor who continually over-estimates his own talent. Getting booted off the bottom-lessly awful *Batman* gravy train was not enough to humble the hunky, talentless slab of beef loin. Perhaps *Moreau* will do the trick. (What am I saying?! Joel Schumacher has produced boatloads of horrible films since *D.C. Cab*, proving once again that in Hollywood, it is not whether you succeed or fail but the magnitude of your success or failure.)

Tapped to add to the confusion was Fairuza Balk, fresh from her bigger-than-life performance in *The Craft*, and David Thewlis, a marvelous actor who really should know better. John Frankenheimer directed, apparently forgetting everything he knew when making *The Manchurian Candidate.*

All things considered, if Everest-sized drifts of the finest Colombian white lady were vacuumed up by cast and crew alike in the making of this film, it wouldn't surprise me at all. Not an accusation, just an observation.

Standing atop this mountain of confusion is Brando himself. The man whose mythic reading of "I swallowed a bug" (sadly cut from *Apocalypse Now*, but seen in the wonderful documentary *Hearts of Darkness*) stretches himself even further. Pale-faced and wearing prosthetic buck teeth and large Bea Arthurian muumuus, he stumbles through a performance as laughable as any since whatever film Arnold Schwarzenegger has just completed. Only the kiss he laid on the ratlike, cadaverous Larry King is more revolting than his performance in *Moreau.*

Let me amend that. Seeing his buttery, corpulent mass oozing around in bed with the 30 percent postconsumer recycled plastic body of Faye Dunaway was as horrible a thing as any man could be asked to endure. Save seeing Chris Farley eat a Frisco meal deal at Hardee's.

That scene, of course, was from *Don Juan De Marco,* another movie I wanted to slap sharply, without apology.

How far back must we travel to find a Brando performance free of laughable eccentricities and doughy backsides? Hard to say. Exempting *A Dry White Season,* it would have to be a very long time indeed. Though he remained mercifully clothed in *Superman,* he truly turned in one of the dumbest performances ever purchased for $80 million, or whatever it was he got paid.

For the making of *Superman* he demanded that he not see his lines before filming, and that they be put on cue cards at all the points he was going to look during the filming of his scenes. This he learned from Stanislavsky by way of Strasberg, in a course called "The Method: Use it to Suck."

Because I want to eat again in my lifetime, and perhaps have intimate relations with a female, I shall not evoke the image of Brando in *Last Tango in Paris.*

Can we expect the kind of behavior and performances that Brando has exhibited from contemporary actors in the future? Must we endure the sight of a three-hundred-pound Skeet Ulrich lolling about in bed with a geriatric Drew Barrymore? Will Woody Harrelson only perform in a Bell helicopter and then demand to be paid in hemp? I think you can count on that one.

As for Brando, when will he stop making films? It's not funny anymore. It hurts.

Just stop it!

Prince *Nikolaus* Esterhazy of Austria was the bene-
factor of one Franz Josef Haydn, the prolific and
brilliant father of the symphonic form and mentor to the
great Beethoven himself. *Joe* Eszterhas is the prolific
screenwriter who has turned out such works as *Sliver* and
Showgirls.

Coincidence? Yes. And not even a very interesting one,
considering their names are spelled differently and
they're not in the same field. Joe Eszterhas is a huge, hairy
bear of a man who lumbers around writing filthy, misogynist screenplays. Prince Esterhazy registered no dirty
screenplays with the Writers Guild, and he at least had the
decency to powder his hair to keep the stink down.

Still, it does clearly illustrate how people with similar-
sounding last names can be cut from a different cloth
entirely. For example, Lynda *Carter* and George Washington *Carver*. Without placing any value judgments on either
person, I think they're quite different, assuming Mr.
Carver didn't own tights and over-the-calf red leather
boots.

To explore the whole subject even further, I perused the Joe Eszterhas oeuvre—no mean feat, and one best left to someone with a high threshold of nausea.

Flashdance (1983) was a seminal work for Eszterhas, blending as it did elements of exploitation, pure stupidity, and soaking-wet women pounding on chairs. *Flashdance* was a huge hit, and now that he's a household name, it's interesting to note that this was one of Michael Nouri's first films.

It starred Jennifer *"The Bride"* Beals as a young woman who was a welder by day (arc welder, I believe; I think it would have weakened her character to have her an oxyacetylene or wire-feed welder) and dancer by night. She danced at an establishment frequented by bulbous, longneck-swilling teamsters who happened to be enthusiasts of muscular, stylized modern dance, all of it done fully clothed. Eszterhas would probably claim that this is satire, but it's important to remember that Eszterhas is a large idiot.

Though Beals welds, cavorts in thongs, and sleeps with her hirsute boss, she really wants to dance with the ballet. She works very hard at it, forgetting the number-one rule of ballet dancers: smoke six packs of Lucky Strikes every day, whether you feel like it or not. Lillian Hellman was in dance training her whole life.

What you really take away from the film is the fact that Jennifer Beals is "a maniac, maniac on the floor. *And,* she's dancing like she's never danced before." Those lyrics always gave me the impression that she had snapped and was mowing down patrons at Alley Gators with an Italian carbine selected from her overstuffed duffel bag.

At the time, some thought the film an abomination, a clear sign of the end times, the opening of the Seventh Seal—while others liked the music and thought it had a lot of "pep." Eszterhas became a huge success and devoted time to looking more like an endomorphic Viking.

He then pursued a course of mediocrity for nine years after *Flashdance* until hitting it big with 1992's smash soft-core/snuff thriller *Basic Instinct,* starring Sharon Stone and Michael "Chin Tuck" Douglas. Eszterhas had always courted controversy with his "frank" and "moronic" screenplays, but *Basic Instinct* was surely his magnum opus. Working on the premise that sex equals death and the whole of the world is populated by sleazy, demonic people in sharp suits and tight sweater-dresses, Eszterhas spun a tale of an icy, bisexual predator, played by the icy, (?)-sexual Sharon Stone, who seduces a loathsome police detective, played by the loathsome, rough-sex specialist Michael Douglas.

Much was made of the shocking, surprise nude-ness of the oft-nude Sharon Stone (she claimed she didn't know it was being filmed), and the fact that a bisexual was portrayed in such a negative light. Demonstrators showed up at the opening of the film to show their displeasure (and perhaps get a glimpse of the hunky Douglas), yet what the demonstrators forgot was that they were protesting a bottomlessly awful movie. If you find something offensive in an episode of, say, *Webster,* it's best to just leave it alone and let the problem disappear by itself.

Surfing the success of *Instinct,* Eszterhas continued to roll with such films as *Sliver, Jade,* and *Showgirls.*

Sliver starred one of those younger, squintier Baldwin brothers, and was essentially the same movie-going experience as *Instinct*, save for the price hike on Junior Mints in the lobby. Ditto *Jade*, except this one starred that gaunt, clown-headed fellow David Caruso, by all accounts an evil, whiny little man, the kind best suited for an Eszterhas outing. *Showgirls* we've all seen and needs no further lucubration from me.

Those who follow his career (pornographers and the like) wonder what Eszterhas will do next? Will he shower? Not likely. Will he stride around Hollywood like a side of beef with whiskers? This is the most probable course. Stay tuned.

There haven't been any Crocodile Dundee films in a while, and it's true that Corey Haim isn't bringing 'em in like he used to, but we mustn't grow complacent. We must remain ever vigilant, eyes open to the future, minds fully aware of our shameful, Molly Ringwald–studded past. Remember, there was a time in this country when Andrew McCarthy could open a movie! I don't blame any single individual, for we're all responsible. And those who didn't lay down their box-office dollars are at least guilty of standing by doing nothing while we showered McCarthy with wealth and adoration, simply for standing in front of a camera like a gaffed salmon, mouthing the words of Bret Easton Ellis and Joel Schumacher.

It will not do to say, "Oh, we were young then, we're so much wiser now." And it certainly won't do to say, "I was so much older then, I'm younger than that now," because that's just silly. Our national hubris is dangerous folly considering that Brad Pitt, a large chunk of butt steak with hair if I ever saw one, sits atop mountains of gold, drinking in the praises of millions. Let's face it, he's the Bay City Rollers of acting.

In order that I may be ready lest another direct McCarthy attack be launched, I reviewed *St. Elmo's Fire* and *Less Than Zero*, suffering greatly, but becoming that much wilier.

Less Than Zero is the 1987 film based on the Bret Easton Ellis novel of the same name. I haven't read the novel, but I do know it's not very good. Although in general I'm opposed to the prejudicial dismissal of any artist's work, in this case I think I'm on pretty safe ground. Someone once begged me to read Jay McInerney's *Bright Lights, Big City*, and, unfortunately, I did. There's an hour and a half I'll never have back.

In *Zero*, McCarthy plays the best friend of Robert Downey, Jr., a hard-partying coke fiend, and amoral loser. (No jokes at the expense of Downey's tragic life. He suffered enough by being in *Chances Are*, with Cybill Shepard.) Jamie Gertz is the woman torn between the volcanic passions of these two thin, pale '80s guys.

The plot is this: Robert Downey, Jr., takes drugs.

It's actually not as gripping as it sounds. I tarted it up for effect. In scene after scene, "Ol' One Expression" McCarthy and "Friend of the Director" Gertz simply try to find the coke-snorting Downey at bad '80s clubs in L.A. It was much easier for me, going to college at a Wisconsin State school—guys were either at Johnny's or the Rathskellar. If Bret Easton Ellis had majored in sociology at UW-Whitewater, it would have saved us all a lot of trouble.

Through it all, McCarthy is typically cadaverous. He is

strangely detached from any scene, looking every bit like a man preoccupied with the fact that his phone bill is so big.

It makes his performance in *St. Elmo's Fire* look downright crackling, which it most assuredly wasn't. *Fire,* of course, is *the* big Brat Pack movie, starring Emilio Estevez, Rob Lowe, Demi Moore, Ally Sheedy, Judd Nelson, Mare Winningham, and of course, Martin Balsam, the unofficial leader of the Brat Pack. I don't know who coined the term "Brat Pack," but the fact that Sinatra didn't have them killed is testament to how much he mellowed over his later years.

St. Elmo's Fire, written and directed by Joel "Man-Goat" Schumacher, is the story of a group of thin, pale '80s guys and gals who have trouble adjusting to life after college and so cope with it by acting like shallow idiots. Even the powerful screen presence of Ally Sheedy cannot save this film. The quiet dignity of Judd Nelson is wasted on the mealy script.

The close-knit camaraderie of the group has produced a kind of celebratory war whoop among them that I believe is supposed to be endearing. But one look at Rob Lowe saying, "Booga booga booga, oo, ha ha ha," and you'll want to never stop hitting him.

McCarthy plays a nihilistic writer secretly in love with his friend's fiancée, played by Ally Sheedy. This he gets right, because if you are in love with Ally Sheedy, you'll want to keep it secret should you ever desire respect from another human being. In McCarthy's world, being nihilistic means smoking, talking kind of fast, and chatting with inexplicably wise hookers. Now that I think of it, that's fairly authentic to the nihilists I know. Throw in smelly and unemployed, and McCarthy's performance starts to look pretty good. I've changed my mind, I like Andrew McCarthy. Contact me through the publisher if you've got a *Weekend at Bernie's II* laserdisc to sell.

Demi and Bruce: national treasures, to be sure. To a country rife with anomie and confusion, they are a stabling influence, and certainly as dear to us as Teflon-coated bullets and behemoth, lawyer-pleasing sport-utility vehicles. They are a strong and visible testament to the kind of personal glory one can attain while *simultaneously* raising a family with only the help of a small squadron of au pairs, nannies, personal trainers, chefs, lawyers, decorators, tutors, stylists, personal assistants, managers, color consultants, guides, pilots, plastic surgeons, body painters, shiatsu masseuses, dog groomers, and spinning instructors.

Certainly when one sees Demi Moore's towering performance in *Striptease,* one feels certain that behind it all is a well-compensated nanny who is comfortable with her benefits package. Though I've never been in such a position, I can only imagine that it's easier to shake your potatoes for the camera when you know your children are snug at home with the lady from the placement agency.

I revisited Moore's oeuvre recently, selecting the Barry

Levinson sex romp *Disclosure* and the saucy Nathaniel Hawthorne potboiler *The Scarlet Letter.*

The Scarlet Letter, as you'll recall from high school (I can't recall, as I was too busy reading *Cracked* magazine), is the story of Hester Prynne and her forbidden love, a love that threatened the repressive Puritans of seventeenth-century Boston. I think. As I said, I've never read it. I do know that in Roland Joffe's version, it's the story of Demi Moore and how "buff" she is. It's the story of how modern doctors, using the new blue laser technology, can incise the dermal and subdermal layers without the need for extensive cauterization, resulting in less visible scars.

At the time of its release, much was made of the movie's blatant disrespect for the source book. Though I'm ill-equipped to comment, I do have to wonder whether the novel contained as much *break dancing* as the movie! And was Dimmesdale a member of the pop group Hanson in the *book* as well?! But I kid irreverent adaptations.

I do have to wonder whether Hawthorne would have wanted as many fully nude sponge baths as there were in the movie. What I mean is, I've no doubt that as a man Hawthorne wanted pretty much nothing but sponge baths, but he probably wouldn't have wanted so many of them depicted in the film version of his book.

Actually, *The Scarlet Letter* isn't nearly as bad as I thought it would be. It's not good, certainly, but despite Moore's predictably wooden performance, it's beautifully shot and occasionally watchable. It's just that it has little to do with *The Scarlet Letter,* if my paper-thin knowledge of the story is to be trusted. It might just as well have been based on the obscure 1978 hydraulic manual *The Movement and Storage of Viscous Industrial Fluids.*

While *Letter* is a better movie, it is somehow less entertaining than the bottomlessly horrible *Disclosure,* starring Moore and rough-sex specialist Michael Douglas.

Based on the Michael Crichton book and directed by Barry *"Diner"* Levinson, *Disclosure* is the story of a hip, Seattle software company full to brimming with dark, hateful little people patrolling the glass-and-steel corridors of their self-made hell, deluding themselves with the belief that they're doing something good for the world even while stuffing their dank, Starbucks-stained Dockers with fistfuls of money that does nothing to quell the aching in their gaunt little souls.

Hmmm. Sounds vaguely familiar.

Not surprisingly, and not that we should care, one of these idiots paws another of these idiots on the job, and the poor, pawed idiot (Douglas) files a lawsuit, causing some sort of wan tension among him and the other idiots at his company.

The "sex scenes," such as they are, will make you glad you have a chapter skip on your DVD player. Watching the reptilian Douglas rub his oily, aging body all over the gristly Moore made me nostalgic for the time I saw two geckos locked in coitus.

While the movie attempts to raise provocative questions about sexual conduct at the workplace, it unfortunately uses Moore's plastic chest and Douglas's liposuctioned backside to make its point. The filmmakers are either blindly stupid, horribly cynical, or irretrievably corrupt.

Speaking of cynical, slap-dab in the middle of all this is the smug, self-proclaimed minister of hip, Dennis Miller, making puerile erection jokes. I suppose they're easier than Goethe references.

While Moore's status as a serious actor is in some little doubt (certainly as long as she continues to make David Caruso–like film choices), *Disclosure* and *The Scarlet Letter* cement Demi's impressive reputation as a woman who will take her clothes off.

One of the side effects of living in a country with such an abundance of freedoms is that occasionally a yahoo butts ahead in the huge buffet line of capitalism and fills his plate to overflowing before he's discovered and sent back to sit with his coarse, rowdy cronies.

Carrot Top is one of those guys, as are Bill Paxton, Tom Arnold, Adam Sandler, and even Alanis Morissette. Some, you don't even mind, 'cause you know they won't stay forever, and it's even kind of fun to have the lovable dopes around. I'm talking about your Hoyt Axtons and your "Weird Al" Yankovics. Others carry the ruse out so long, you don't even stop to think that they've been on the dole the entire time. Ed McMahon and Jimmy Buffett come immediately to mind.

Yet none has perpetrated as perfect a scheme as the phenomenally below-average Keanu Reeves. Daily, the little twerp pulls truckloads of wool over the fawning eyes of billions of Americans who, after emptying their wallets, give him their cash cards and PIN numbers as well. This is a man you rent skis from, not someone you point a camera at for the purpose of entertaining the masses. At best, he's a piece of scenery. At worst, he's not quite as effective as sandbags in your backseat for winter traction.

After viewing *Point Break,* the film where *Patrick Swayze out-acts him!!!,* and *Speed,* where he managed to look more stoned than Dennis Hopper, I propose that we simply put him out to stud.

Point Break, as you'll recall, is one of the triumvirate of Patrick Swayze vehicles that established him as kind of a smaller, slightly brighter model of Jean-Claude Van Damme. (The others are *Next of Kin* and *Road House.* They are best viewed one after the other, with no breaks in a beery, Old Milwaukee haze.) In it, Keanu plays a hot-shot FBI agent who must learn to surf in order to track a group of hotdogging bank robbers who do it for the adrenaline rush. (Presumably *Surge* was created to quell the swelling rate of "extreme" bank robberies perpetrated by annoying suburban kids in phat pants.)

Keanu Reeves is as convincing as an FBI agent as he would be playing William Howard Taft. In my day, we had Efrem Zimbalist, Jr., as an FBI agent, and we were damn happy for it! Now any Slurpee-guzzling hobbledehoy can don a fake badge and chase after brigands and malefactors!

Reeves always looks out of place when he has to say words, a detriment to an actor, in my opinion. Phrases like "let's go" and "over here" sound forced and wooden.

He fares only slightly better in *Speed,* I'm afraid to say, allowing himself to be blown off the screen by Jeff Daniels, Sandra Bullock, and a bus. I think he'd be wise to do summer stock opposite heavy machinery for a couple of years until he gets his sea legs. Perhaps *The Odd Couple*, starring Reeves and a Caterpillar lift truck. Or *Arsenic and Old Lace*, with a front-end loader and a late-model Peterbilt.

In *Speed*, Keanu plays a member of the Los Angeles bomb squad who is forced by an evil madman, Dennis "One-Hitter" Hopper, to drive a bus wired to blow up should its speed fall below fifty miles an hour. Once again, Keanu Reeves—member of the Los Angeles bomb squad!? I wouldn't trust this man to sell me a stamp. He's the type of guy who I always get helping me at RadioShack. He's the night stock boy at Target.

As bad as he is, Reeves comes out smelling like a rose compared with the scenery-chewing THC receptacle that is Dennis Hopper. His run as the go-to villain in every bad action movie has got to come to an end, even if it means letting Eric Roberts have a turn now and then.

If you haven't seen *Speed* yet, don't. But if you must, I warn you: It's one of those movies that tricks you into thinking it's over long before it actually is. Just when you're running for the exits, cursing yourself for not having seen *Cool Runnings* or *Beethoven's 2nd*, it starts all over with a newer, stupider plot line! It's the cinematic equivalent of a 401K meeting that goes right through lunch.

If you're still having doubts about Reeves's little joke at our expense, I recommend you rent *Dangerous Liaisons* (a good movie, save Reeves), *A Walk in the Clouds,* and *Chain*

Reaction. When you're done, watch them again, only this time, tape a six-inch piece of two-by-four to your screen and imagine it's Reeves. I guarantee you'll prefer the two-by-four every time. I've tested it on my friends, and it really works. Enjoy!

DVD is the technology that brings together digital sound and picture, allowing the viewer to become involved in *Spandau Ballet Live!* or James Belushi's *K-9* like never before. In a moment, I'll take a look at the latest software, but first, I thought it appropriate to say a few words about the much-maligned, and finally failed, Divx technology.

Divx (pronounced DI-vix or duh-VIX or DIVE-x or DUH-vuhzz) allowed the consumer to give all their financial information and entertainment preferences to a shadowy organization *over the phone lines.* Additionally consumers could expect to spend even more time shopping for Divx at one of the many soothing Circuit City superstores. Divx would have been a boon to those who drop by their area Best Buy just to relax and say "howdy" to their friends and neighbors on a regular basis. I personally log quite a few hours at my neighborhood Office Max, just shooting the breeze, sharing harmless gossip with the local staff, or merely drinking in the simple country wisdom that seems to ooze from the place.

Technologically, Divx was similar to DVD except that all Divx releases were "pan and scan." While it might be a considered advantage to see less of Tim Allen in *Jungle2Jungle*, there are those rare movies where one likes to see the whole screen. Here, Divx disappointed. On the plus side, Divx allowed only forty-eight hours to view the film once it was put in the player. Now, if your child brought home *Son in Law* with Pauly Shore, I can't imagine a scenario where unlimited viewings would be desired. In such a case, the limits of Divx were actually a plus.

Clearly, the idea was that DVD and Divx could coexist in the same market, with the savvy consumer coming down on the side of DVD, and the hopeless, gullible, and staggeringly dense consumer siding with Divx. But I kid the failed technology.

As a poignant example of the DVD advantage, I recently rented Carrot Top's *Chairman of the Board* in glorious wide screen! Though both pan and scan and wide were available on the same disc, I felt certain his beta-carotene-rich head would be lost in certain scenes unless viewed as the director intended. I wanted to give every chance to Carrot, because trashing Carrot Top has become a national sport for everyone who isn't Carrot Top.

In *Chairman of the Board*, Mr. Top plays a down-on-his-luck inventor who, during the course of a day, does a good turn for an unbelievably rich CEO, played by Jack Warden. Predictably, Warden dies almost immediately after his day with Carrot Top; unsurprising, as I myself spent merely ninety minutes with Carrot Top and was praying for my own death. Warden, of course, leaves his company to Top. This enrages the heir apparent, Warden's nephew, played by Larry Miller, who then plots to undermine Top, with the help of a rival company owner, played by Raquel Welch, who is now made from 50 percent postconsumer recycled parts.

Carrot Top himself is a performer who defies categorization. Is he an idiot or merely a moron? Does he make me nauseous, or simply headachy and kind of sad? Do I want to hit him in the face with a sack of flour, or in the groin with a Wiffle bat? Yes, sad to say, I'm joining the great choir of voices engaging in the empty sport of Carrot Top bashing.

For there is nothing sadder than a comedian bombing. Several levels of hell below that is a prop comedian bombing. All prop comedians, viewed outside the very specific frame they have set for themselves, look like sad, sick little children craving love they can never have. No one wants to hug a prop comedian. *Chairman of the Board* is essentially this scenario encased in an easy-to-view movie form!

One particularly ironic moment in the film is when Top and his two misfit roommates buy a crate of John Tesh CDs and use them for trapshooting. This is something akin to seeing Three-Stooge Shemp Howard make fun of Mortimer Snerd. Or, say, a garden slug insulting the intelligence of a mealworm.

The DVD format allowed for some decent extras on *C.O.T.B.,* including an interview with the star, a rock video, and, yes, *commentary on the making of the film by Carrot Top himself!!* I admit I didn't listen to the entire thing, but I listened long enough to hear these observations by Top. "Uh-oh," followed by a minute of silence. "This part is really funny," followed by several minutes of silence. And, "This scene was really hard to film, 'cause I was nude!"

Divx could never offer that! Get yourself a DVD player—see Carrot Top nude. You owe it to yourself.

In the bitter cold of the north, where I make my home, the winds can numb your hands, making even the simplest of tasks, like switching off Garrison Keillor or returning the latest Prince CD, a painful and difficult chore. We depend on our vehicles here. Whether it be a trip out to buy another puffy, unattractive coat, or to mail more rambling, incoherent letters to the local paper about the incompetence of the Vikings' coaching staff, we demand rugged reliability from our automobiles. Legends are born out of these harsh conditions. Legends with names like Dodge *Shadow* and Hyundai *Sonata*. Names that calm and comfort with their silent strength, like GMC *Jimmy* and Chevrolet *1T Cube Conversion Van*. Personally I rely on the Jeep *Cherokee*, a vehicle that, if you discount the replaced head gasket, the snapped rear-door support, the various brake and coolant line leaks, the noisy, unreliable ABS pump, the poor gas mileage, the shockingly bumpy ride, and the horrible ergonomics, has *never* let me down.

Bruce Willis is like my Jeep.

Let's face it, we bought Bruce Willis because we

thought he was rugged and dependable. Since that time, we've had no end of trouble with him. He's got a bad ABS pump, a snapped rear-door support, bead leaks on virtually every tire—he's proven a bad purchase. And he's not becoming more lovable and etched with character over time, like your dad's old Chevy. *Again,* he's like my Jeep, where the paint is coming off in huge chips, and the rust is spreading around all the sheet metal screws, making it look like the kind of vehicle an unsuccessful check-forger might drive.

If my tortured analogy has done nothing else, I hope it has at least shown you that Bruce Willis is very like a rusty 4X4 driven by a petty criminal somewhere in Minnesota or western Wisconsin.

Nothing could illustrate that fact more clearly than his recent offering, *Mercury Rising*. Willis stars as Art Jeffries, a reprimanded FBI agent who must protect an autistic child from the ruthless head of the NSA, played by Alec Baldwin. The NSA, it turns out, has created a new, impenetrable code that protects foreign security agents better than the older, more penetrable one. In order to test it, they publish it in a typical grocery store puzzle book, and it's immediately solved by a nine-year-old autistic boy named Simon. Since it would be almost prohibitively expensive to write a newer, even less penetrable code, the NSA decides to keep Mercury, as it's called, and instead, kill Simon and his whole family. Apparently the killing budget of NSA is lavish, or else there was plenty of escrow.

It's the kind of stupid, implausible movie that Willis is supposed to excel in, and yet, this time his pained, raisiny face simply looks tired. It's entirely plausible that simple domestic tedium is responsible for his lackluster showing on-screen—perhaps the guy to fix the boiler was there right as Bruce was supposed to drive the kids to piano lessons. Could be there were nights, after long hours of shooting, when Bruce had to work on refinishing that chest of drawers for the extra room. Maybe Maria Shriver was in for an emergency hair enlargement, and Bruce had to watch the kids so that Arnold could be with her. Sure, these could be contributing factors, yet I think it much more likely that he has stopped focusing on his film work and become *much more focused on chicken finger sell-through at his growing chain of franchised theme restaurants!* Yes, part-ownership in Planet Hollywood has killed his slightly-more-than-mediocre film career.

I for one feel cheated. This was never the case with John Wayne, Clint Eastwood, or even Ben Gazzara. These are men who wouldn't be caught dead selling appetizers and foo-foo drinks to doughy tourists in big shorts. These are tough men who've never even requested potential franchise literature from Chili's or TGI Fridays, let alone opened their own gaudy, tasteless mall eateries that give away balloons and serenade you on your birthday. The places where these men of action eat have no pictures of the food on huge, laminated menus. They eat good, wholesome meals served by women named Vy and Thelma, not cutesy burger plates served by guys with their hats on backward, with names like Todd and Justin. Ben Gazzara has never sold a single potato skin to anyone in his life.

It's time for Willis to shape up and use his large, rugged head to fill up screen space in big, dumb movies, not concern himself with linen supply companies and ice-cube makers. If he does not, I shall be forced to revisit my Willis-Jeep analogy, and no one wants that.

PART EIGHT

VERY ODDS 'N' ENDS

THE CRAFT

Satan has been involved in the film industry for many years, but 1996's *The Craft* would have to be his most personal film. Because it involved subjects so dear to him (corruption, darkness, hate), Old Goosberry assembled the hottest young actors and one of his most trusted directors to pull the project together. Though uncredited, it's widely acknowledged that the Arch-Fiend worked closely with the creative team from the beginning all the way through the screening process, suggesting changes, penning rewrites himself—even hosting creative meetings at his summer place overlooking the River Styx. "I'd been wanting to work with Skeet Ulrich for some time," The Author of All Lies told Mary Hart. "This just seemed like the perfect project."

The Craft begins as young Sarah and her barely sentient father move into a spooky old mansion in a trendy section of Los Angeles. Minutes after arriving, a smelly, unshowered man shows up, mumbles something, and leaves a snake on their floor. Sarah screams, most likely unaware that in L.A., at least three times a week, a smelly, unshowered man will show up, mumble, and leave *something* on your floor. A snake is actually the most common item, and probably the safest.

Her first day at her new school, she runs afoul of the "Bitches of Eastwick" (named after the John Updike novelization of the Michelle Pfeiffer film), three unpopular girls who turned to witchcraft when their chunky Skechers shoes failed to impress their classmates. (Though they're consistently referred to as trashy and dirty, they appear hygenic and well dressed to my eyes—certainly no worse than Elizabeth Montgomery.) When the three, Nancy, Bonnie, and Rochelle, discover that Sarah has the power to make a pencil stand on its end, they recruit her for the coven, offering a generous benefits package and a company broom. She signs with them, and they're off to the local witch supply store, Affiliated Witch and Diabolism, where they encourage Sarah to shoplift evil sundries using the justification "Everything in nature steals, you know." Not to be punctilious, but I think it's fairly easy to come up with many examples of things in nature that don't steal: Aardwolves, they don't steal. Kelp would be another example. Yeast. Pumice. Lithium salts, never been known to steal. Aphids. I could go on, but I think the point is clear: Don't use wholly inaccurate generalizations of the natural world as a basis for your moral framework. When deciding whether or not to commit insurance fraud, don't rely on the advice of friends who say, "You know everything in nature, especially sandpipers, commits insurance fraud."

Soon after they leave the store, Sarah is confronted by Snake Guy again. This time, he chases after her mumbling a vague prophecy, and when he is hit by a car and killed, the girls thank their god, Manon. Sarah is ignorant of Manon, so Nancy (Fairuza Balk) explains, "If God and the Devil were playing football, Manon would be the sun that shone down on them." The answer satisfies Sarah, who goes about worshiping Manon, but it left some questions in my mind. For instance, What if it was a night game or was being played in a domed stadium? And why football? What is specific to football that makes it the best analogy for illustrating the character of Manon? Would "lacrosse" have failed to convey some key piece of Manon's essence? I must remember not to spend too much time dissecting any philosophy uttered by a person named Fairuza.

As their power in Manon grows, the girls begin exacting their evil revenge on anyone who ever slighted them. Nancy uses a spell to kill her stepfather; Sarah, to humiliate her boyfriend; while Rochelle uses it to depilate the head of a girl who insulted her, making her hair look like a scabby tonsure. It's frankly pretty unimpressive stuff from the guy who is the sun over the God-Devil football matchup. It could be that Manon's job as Ballgame Sun really limits his powers in other areas.

Sarah grows frightened of the turn their evil magic is taking, and so consults the woman at the witch supply store, who tells her, "True magic is neither black nor white. It's both because nature is both—loving and cruel at the same time." I guess the witch store also provides bullshit watered-down pantheism as well. Does she really expect us to believe that if a rival witch-store owner uses magic to crash her Cavalier through the front window and steal all of her eye of newt *and* her pricey grease that's sweated from the murderer's gibbet, she'd conclude that it's "neither black nor white"?

The rest of the coven, sensing Sarah's potential to rebel, tries to kill her. She runs back to the witch-store owner, who takes her to the supply room, where she has a big satanic temple set up. Because of deleted scenes, sloppy editing, or some censoring by Manon, nothing happens in the big satanic temple. Instead, we cut to Sarah's house, where maggots, snakes, and lizards appear on her patio. Sounds like a typical Hollywood party to me! (Ha ha ha, ha . . . ha . . . well, anyway.) Sarah screams and runs, only to find her toilet crammed to the rim with roaches and scorpions. I can tell you from experience, the first time you see your toilet crammed with roaches and scorpions, it can be a bit off-putting. The trick is not to get into one of those I-can-wait-longer-than-you-can things with your roommates—just bite the bullet and *clean* the thing.

In the end, Sarah's slightly less offensive brand of satanism wins out, though it's unclear whether that's supposed to make us happy, sad, indifferent, or just logy.

The Craft is the kind of movie that makes you wonder if we shouldn't just take a couple years off from movies and play badminton instead. It's packed with all those Neve Campbells and Skeet Ulrichs (who should be held accountable for the crap they help to make), and it glorifies witchcraft and satanism and targets the vulnerable teen crowd.

Frankly, I expected better things from Satan.

DATE WITH AN ANGEL/ MY DEMON LOVER

It's hard to remember now, nearly ten years later, how deeply gripped by *Mannequin* fever this country really was. The 1987 Andrew McCarthy–Kim Cattrall film captivated a nation desperate to forget the fact that they had allowed a Rick Springfield song to hit the top of the charts. I was in college at the time (or, to be fastidiously honest, had been kicked out of college for low grades and was working as a janitor) and remember how profoundly affected I was by the lowbrow paranormal sexfarce. I realize, in retrospect, the effect was quite inflated by the six-pack of warm Schaeffer beer I had downed in the theater parking lot, yet, still in all, the movie was quite popular, and it's reasonable to assume that the entire nation wasn't potted when they made *Mannequin* a runaway hit.

The high-spirited romp *Date with an Angel* sets out to prove that the messengers of the Lord are equally adept as day players in farcical send-ups as they are trumpeting the word of the Almighty to the quaking masses. Michael E. Knight (Tad Martin of *All My Children*) stars as Jim, a musician/composer/loser who is engaged to Patty, a shrill, shallow irritant played quite convincingly by the shrill and shallow Phoebe Cates. Jim is shanghaied from his engagement party by a trio of shockingly annoying "friends" and brought to a hollow bacchanalia that is to pass for his bachelor party. It is there that the Angel (played, sort of, by Emmanuelle Beart), who apparently hasn't filed a flight plan with Gabriel, crashes into Jim's pool, picking up a green-stick fracture in her left dorsal wing. The grounded seraphim is put on the fifteen-day DL, but is expected to take the rubber in the Cleveland series, provided the X rays on the rotator cuff look clean. What I mean to say is, she just sort of hangs out with Jim, annoying his affianced, while Patty's dad and Jim's triumvirate of loser friends attempt to kidnap her for immoral purposes.

Bottom line: It's not very good. But who's at fault, the makers of *Date with an Angel,* or me, who, to exclusion of other, more healthy things, sat home on a Saturday night watching the Michael E. Knight movie *Date with an Angel?*

My Demon Lover tells the charming story of a filthy, scorbutic homeless man, Kaz, who becomes possessed by the devil every time he gets, ahem, aroused. How did they sell that in the pitch meeting, you ask? Two words: Scott Valentine. As Justine Bateman's wood-headed boyfriend on the mythically popular *Family Ties,* Mr. Valentine made the phrase "Yo, Mallory" resonate throughout the nation. (I once made a "Yo, Mallory" joke in reference to *Morte D'Arthur* that was coolly received by my fellow janitors.)

Michelle Little is Kaz's girlfriend, Denny, who invites

you to enjoy her $1.99 Grand Slam Breakfast. Denny learns early on in their relationship that Old Gooseberry bunks out in her boyfriend's soul, but she doesn't seem to mind; au contraire, she even offers to arouse the Archfiend to test Kaz's theory that he is The Mangler. The Mangler murders women by, well, mangling them. I think it was one of the smaller newspapers in town that gave him the name.

Kaz is not The Mangler. The Mangler is actually another man possessed by demons, the milquetoast Charles, played by . . . oh, who cares? Charles and Kaz do battle on the parapets of a castle set conveniently in a movie studio. In the end, he gets the girl and is no longer possessed by demons. It's sort of *The Exorcist* meets *The Pick-Up Artist*.

Which one would I bring on a desert island? I'd have to say *Date with an Angel*. It's slightly longer, and because I wouldn't have AC power on this desert island and wouldn't be able to watch the movie, anyway, I'd have more tape to fashion into a crude sling with which to kill the indigenous gulls, roasting their still-trembling bodies on the coals of dried pimento branches I had saved for the occasion, crushing the bitter berries of the low regional shrubs and using them for flavoring.

Character. That's what high school football is all about. Finding your own limits, pushing yourself—building character.

And giving the skinny kid double jock locks and power sit-ups. And there's the extremely personal, wholly devastating taunts to inflict on anyone outside the clique. And there's lots of lemon-flavored vodka to be drunk.

If I sound bitter, it's because my participation in high school football ended after two weeks when a teammate relieved himself in my locker. His action was condoned and encouraged by the coach, a mean little man with a goatee who seemed to enjoy the smell of jockstraps. This same man once threw a basketball full force at my bare back for some imagined infraction. And it was he who gave a speech in which he claimed he could break our arms if he felt like it and not have to worry because he'd purchased insurance for just that purpose. (I believe New York Life offers High School Kid Arm Breaking Coverage in several different packages, depending on whether you also want to kick the child as well.) It smelled suspiciously like a stock speech, one probably found in *Petty Tyranny: A Comprehensive Handbook for Gym Coaches.*

I'm trying once again to advance my theory that gym teachers and high school football coaches are solely responsible for all the evil in the world. Yes, all darkness is brought about not by Satan, the *alleged* author of all lies, or any other supernatural force, but by middle-aged men in Russell athletic shorts who have big guts and bald shins. Men who wish they'd had the smarts to get into the Marines. Barrel-chested fellows who call young men "ladies" and who shout disingenuous statements of incredulity like, "I do not BELIEVE what I am SEEING here, ladies." You see, I think they do believe what they are seeing. It's the dishonesty I can't stand. Well, that and the thick hairs that sprout from their ears.

Varsity Blues, a film that features Jon Voight as just such a tyrannical coach, attempts to expose the inner workings of the high school football system of a small town in Texas. In my opinion, live and let live, especially in the case of Texans. They are well armed, have drive-up liquor stores, and are very enthusiastic about the death penalty.

The film opens by introducing us to its cast of zany characters, which are really like plain-label generic characters meant to provide a better value than their full-priced equivalents. There's the obese party animal, Billy Bob; the randy party animal, Tweeder; our hero, Moxon (it took some moxie to give him that precious name); and the star quarterback, Lance Harbor. Why not just go all the way and name the guy Hard Chestslab or Jack Rockback?

The West Canaan Coyotes are going for their twenty-third division title led by their tough, unforgiving coach,

Jack Evilcoach. No, wait, it's Bud Kilmer. Jon Voight, as Kilmer, holds nothing back and at times is not just eating scenery but vacuuming up huge amounts of it with Eric Roberts–like zeal. Come to think of it, Voight didn't really go off the rails as an actor until he worked with Roberts in *Runaway Train*. I hope he doesn't work with Adam Sandler anytime soon.

The Coyotes are a shoo-in to go undefeated, until quarterback Strong Chunkrip gets injured and our Hero, Moxon (James Van Der Beek), has to go in for him. Moxon saves the day, and so Fist Strongpunch's girlfriend tries to seduce him while still in the hospital, just after seeing Stone Irongrip's X rays! The girlfriend, played by Tiffany Love (can you believe the names?), is one of the more disturbing elements of the film. Her character, at seventeen years old, spends one-third of the film naked, another third naked and having sex on a washing machine, and the other third delicately clothed in whipped cream attempting to seduce Moxon. She makes Shannon Tweed look like a frigid 1890s schoolmarm. Now, the difficulties of getting whipped cream to stay put on a warm body aside, this character doesn't speak well of the filmmaker's view on women. Fans of the film may try to defend it by pointing out that Moxon's girlfriend is virginal and represents a kind of morality, which they'd do quickly because the whipped cream scene was coming up again. But in the film's world, "virginal" means slightly smaller breasts. Not a single kid is awkward or pimply or sexually inexperienced. Everyone is freakishly self-possessed and uncommonly mature. It troubles me because I'm not there yet myself.

Getting back to the plot, Moxon as the new star quarterback becomes a full-fledged celebrity in West Canaan. Kids want his autograph, girls want to wear whipped cream for him, crusty old grocers give him free Budweiser (too cheap to go with Lone Star, I guess). At one point, he takes his friends to a strip club, where they discover their voluptuous sex-education teacher is one of the dancers! Oh, no! That's so naughty! It's like a Van Halen song fully realized. They pull a Mickey Rourke and drink at the dingy club till seven in the morning, losing their next game because even hours later, their blood is 20 percent watermelon-flavored gin.

Despite the loss, they go on to play for the state championship, which, as you might imagine, involves a lot of *Henry V*–style we-few-we-happy-few speeches and super-slow-motion photography. Sandwiched in there somewhere is a subplot about racism that asserts boldly that blacks can play football every bit as good as whites.

Varsity Blues has many flaws, among them the fact that it's not very good. Plus it depicts every adult as either evil or stupid. There are the obscene parodies of Southerners as kind of mentally unbalanced *Hee-Haw* outcasts. And a little brother who straps himself to a cross and wears it around the house. Later he buys condoms for his older brother. Then he forms a death cult. The teen girls are almost always naked and about to have sex. The boys are all brutish alcoholic thugs.

In short, it's kind of offensive, but it does accurately convey the feeling of elation one gets upon vanquishing one's foe in a mighty test of courage and will. I think. I've personally never been on the winning end of any sporting event I've participated in. Okay, once I bested my opponents in a particularly savage cakewalk in the third grade. The chilling presence of coaches has kept me from every other kind of organized sport.

Those of you who share my feelings on coaches, rest assured, I'll be out there, like Van Helsing, trying to put a stop to their evil designs. In the meantime, keep watching the gyms! For God's sake, keep watching the gyms!

"The name's Roger, but you can call me Fuzzy," says the guy who comes to look at my furnace. Well, no, I don't want to you call you Fuzzy. First of all, that would mean saying the word "fuzzy" to another adult human being. And second, it's not your name. Your parents went to a lot of trouble to give you your name—sure, they came up a little short with "Roger," but it's not an easy job. The person who gave you the nickname "Fuzzy" was most likely half drunk at the time and you accepted the name only because you were fully drunk.

I know it's my problem, but I have a hard time with nicknames, of being asked to accept at face value that someone's name is "Stretch" or "Jingle," "Tweety" or "The Stroke." When a person refers to someone by his nickname and the nicknamed accepts it, the transaction robs both parties of dignity. In most cases the moniker is an open sign of disrespect: e.g., you get caught picking your nose by your sophomore classmates, you're nicknamed "Digger." This is not something to propagate. Even in the case of a seemingly innocuous nickname, there is a tacit diminution of your stature; e.g., you work for a factory that does metal plating and your job is to galvanize machine parts, so your friends start calling you "The Dipper." Not offensive, perhaps, but it is reductive. Yes, I do spend some of my time coating machine parts in a solution of zinc, but that isn't *all* I do. Of course you could argue that if your name is Peter, "Peter" isn't all you do, either, but that would be silly.

Even worse is when the nickname is wholly contrived by the person himself. Larry Anderson owns Anderson Meats and Poultry, so he dubs himself Larry "The Meat-Man" Anderson. Larry invites the inherent diminishing nature of his sobriquet. "All I do is meat," says Larry to the world at large. "I don't laugh or cry, sleep or hug my children. I'm simply a medium through which animal flesh is delivered to others."

Given my stance on nicknames, I approached *Patch Adams* cautiously, poking it with a stick first, retreating a few steps and then poking it again. *Patch*, as you may know, is the story of Hunter "Patch" Adams, a physician who perceived a general dissatisfaction with doctor-patient relations and misconstrued that as permission to put on a clown nose and frighten children. It's best never to align yourself with clowns, even in a superficial manner. As my four-year-old son put it after having clowns explained to him, "So clowns are supposed to be funny, but then they accidentally make you sad and afraid?"

The movie opens as Patch checks himself into a psychiatric ward in order to overcome his depression and thoughts of suicide, brought on, no doubt, by feelings that his self-conferred handle is not the smash he thought it would be. One of his first acts is to try to help his room-mate, who is incapacitated by a fear of imaginary squir-rels. Patch begins blowing their imaginary heads off with his imaginary gun, never stopping to think that a deeply unstable man may not be comforted by the sight of exploding squirrel heads. It does briefly distract the man from his psychosis, and so emboldened by his moderate success with squirrel mutilation therapy, Patch decides to enroll in medical school with the dream of someday decapitating real rodents for his own patients.

Once in medical school, he butts heads immediately with the cartoonishly evil dean of the medical school and with his creepy roommate Mitch, played by the creepy guy from *Boogie Nights*. The problem is that no one enjoys Patch's antics as much as Patch, who thinks that hanging upside down from a streetlight and frightening old women establishes his maverick nature and rich sense of humor. He begins stalking beautiful young Carin (Julia Roberts simulacrum Monica Potter), who has the good sense not to fall for his grating shenanigans. Quite fairly rejected by every adult who meets him, he parades his stale act before sick children who laugh dutifully as he recreates Howie Mandel's famous "rubber glove routine." Later, he creeps into a terminally ill man's room and begins "amusing" him with balloon animals. I think we can say with some certainty that anyone who's ever seen a balloon animal act is thinking, somewhere in the back of his mind, how nice it would be to die. For a terminally ill person watching it, the longing for death has to be nearly unbearable.

He brags to a fellow student that he's "really getting

through to these people. Patients are sharing their fantasies with me." This is not something to be encouraged, especially if the word "naughty" is used in any context. There are perfectly serviceable 1-900 numbers for anyone wanting to share their fantasies. It's unseemly for a physician to solicit them, especially if he's charging $3.75 a minute beyond his regular rate.

Patch continually badgers another terminal patient, Bill (Peter Coyote), until, fatigued, he resigns himself to letting Patch amuse himself in his room. When the moment comes for him to step into The Great Beyond, his wife and children excuse themselves so that Patch can send Bill off with a crappy subvaudevillian routine still ringing in his ears. When it's *my* turn to pass, I'm going to shoo my beloved wife and beautiful children from the room and let Gallagher do his stuff! Though he consistently makes the claim that he wants to help people, it's quite obvious he simply wants to do his act before an audience that can't run.

Having had enough, Evil-Dean makes what I thought was a reasonable attempt to have him thrown out of medical school, but Patch appeals to a superior and is reinstated. In retribution, Evil-Dean puts him in charge of welcoming a large group of distinguished gynecologists to the campus. That rapscallion Patch does so by positioning huge papier-mâché legs in such a way that the committee is greeted at the main entrance by the appearance of female genitalia. Hooray for Patch! Women's health is something to be mocked and laughed at! When no none finds it funny, Patch concludes that everyone but he is lacking a sense of humor. The correct conclusion, of course, is that Patch is an unfunny misogynist with loud pants.

Despite his obviously hostile nature, Patch's persistence wears Carin down, and she agrees to see him. Patch immediately takes advantage of her good nature and puts her to work at his poorly run, totally illegal hospital, which he operates out of an old cabin. She makes a midnight house call to one of their depressed patients and finds him sitting at the piano playing Beethoven's *Fur Elise*. Men sitting alone playing *Fur Elise* are never to be trusted, always to be avoided. Their goal is to trick women into believing them to be sensitive and fragile, and they do so without the heavy lifting of actually having to learn a technically challenging song. Their intent is never pure. Should you hear the familiar E, D# repetition and you see anyone but an eleven-year-old girl at the piano, run. Run while you still can. Unfortunately, Carin does not live to heed this advice but is murdered by the duplicitous pianist. (His intent was certainly more nefarious than any other *Fur Elise* player I have ever known, but still, avoid them.)

Despondent, Patch gives up on medical school. In his sorrow, he tells a friend, "In the whole of the animal kingdom, only man kills his own species." You hate to kick a man when he's down, but you're quite wrong, future doctor Hunter "Patch" Adams. I think the Black Widow Spider Council would have something to say about that.

Just when you're cheering his imminent departure, Patch has a change of heart and returns to fulfill an old woman's fantasy of wading into a pool of cooked spaghetti. This is as important as the *Fur Elise* thing: Never, ever fulfill an old woman's fantasy of wading into a pool of spaghetti. In fact, unless you're an old man, never fulfill any old woman's fantasy, even if it's as innocent as meeting Monty Hall. Just to be on the safe side, never fulfill anyone's fantasy, ever.

He still has to overcome yet another dismissal from medical school, which he does by making speech after maudlin speech to a review board that is apparently very susceptible to maudlin speeches. Having soaked up his routine, the committee chairperson delivers a stock McCloud speech. Given by Chief Clifford at the end of every *McCloud* episode ever produced, it usually went like this: "McCloud, you wrecked thirteen police cars, sank the commissioner's yacht, exposed yourself to the city council, stole the mayor's best pair of saddle shoes, and cost the city over four hundred thousand dollars in oats. You're a disgrace to this force . . . good job, McCloud!"

Patch finishes his schooling and graduates with honors as everyone on the planet cheers him and schmaltzy music plays loudly. The pathetic thing about the whole endeavor is that it was partially written by the actual Patch Adams. He even shows up on the DVD version in a documentary on the making of *Patch*. He appears to be a gruff and horrible little man with a Salvador Dali-an mustache and a Jimmy Buffett–type shirt. (You don't suppose that among his many other flaws he might also be a Parrot Head?!) Can you have a titanic ego and also have a waxy handlebar mustache? Evidence to contradict your own lofty conclusions about yourself would greet you in the mirror every day. And then there's the whole "call me 'Patch' " thing. I don't want to indulge your little "Patch" fantasy. It's similar to the dilemma of going to a restaurant and finding that the item you want has a goofy name. I want some food and my dignity; I don't want to order a Double Wet Willie Burger with Pecos Fries.

I'd like to announce a little name change. Everyone but "Patch" Adams can still call me Mike, but I'd like him to call me "Frenchie Poodle-Buns" Nelson. Thanks.

BLAST FROM THE PAST

The year is 1962. Fidel Castro, fearing the world will laugh at his vaudevillian beard and cigar, allows Soviet Premier Nikita Khrushchev to place nuclear-capable missiles on Cuban soil. Khrushchev is himself smarting from the taunts of many leaders who openly refer to him as "that huge, gray baby." American president John F. Kennedy rolls off Judith Campbell and snaps into action. "It shall be the policy of this nation to regaahd any nuclear missile launched from Cuber against any nation in the Western Hemahsphere as an act of wah against the United States," he tells a tense nation. Experts debate whether "Cuber" is actually "Cuba" or if he perhaps mispronounced "tuber," a theory that gathers very little support as intelligence reports show no potatoes possessing nuclear arms. Reporters at the press conference goad the president into saying, "Paaahk ya' caaah by the gaahdan," and everyone laughs.

After meeting with advisors, Kennedy decides to initiate a naval quarantine zone around Cuba, completely cutting off Castro's borscht supply. He hopes this will buy more time for scientists to finish development of their Synthetic Incendiary and Explosive Cigar (SEIC), a technology that until then had been the stuff of cartoons. Fortunately, Khrushchev relents and withdraws the missiles, knowing that any further escalation could lead to nuclear engagement and a total disruption of his meal schedule.

From this historic episode, the film *Blast from the Past* imagines a fiction in which husband and wife Calvin and Helen Weber (Christopher Walken and Sissy Spacek) retreat into a bomb shelter and stay for thirty-five years, mistakenly believing that a nuclear holocaust has indeed taken place. The pregnant Helen gives birth, and they raise their son, Adam, beneath the earth, completely unaware that he will turn out to be Brendan Fraser.

As they hide below the surface, the '60s slip by. Fortunately for the Webers, they completely avoid having to hear a single note of Creedence Clearwater Revival. The '70s pass. No one in the Webers' bunker at any time says the word "dyn-o-mite." The '80s disappear into history, and with it any chance of seeing *Head of the Class*. Adam is raised on old-fashioned values, is taught to dance, box, and learns all about baseball. In short, he's a dope. A moron. A total square. It's the '90s, and Huey Lewis's theory that "it's hip to be square" has been disproved. The only thing we can say with any certainty is that it's not hip to be Huey Lewis.

After an ill-fated trip to the surface on reconnaissance, Calvin has a heart attack, so they send Adam to the surface to get supplies. He botches the job immediately and gets hopelessly lost, proving once again that you simply can't trust guys raised in bunkers beneath the earth. Realizing he'll need more money than he has, he tries to sell off his baseball card collection and is aided by kindly stranger Eve (Alicia Silverstone). Adam falls for her immediately, apparently unaware that she was in *Batman & Robin* and, telling her a lie about living in remote Alaska, asks her to help him buy supplies.

Thus begins a love affair destined for tepidity and luke-warmedness. Eve shuns Adam at first, finding his earnest nature almost as annoying as his performance in *Encino Man,* so he asks for help in finding him a mate. (Had he not lied about the Alaska thing but simply stated up front that he needed a woman to bring back to his bunker, it would have been the first successful use of that line since Hitler in 1945.) She agrees, but then discovers that she loves Adam herself. When he reveals the truth about himself, she tries to have him committed. (This is a scenario so familiar to me. In trying to be open and honest, I once revealed to a date that I constantly heard the voices of Wayland Flowers and Madame chattering away in my head. Once I had extricated myself from the Elk River Psychiatric Ward, I can assure you I didn't call her for a second date.)

Blast from the Past starts off strong, with funny performances by Sissy Spacek and Christopher Walken, who could play the Dalai Lama and still appear as though he were about to snap. But the whole thing is hampered by the awkward love story between Fraser and Silverstone (not to take anything away from her superior nonstick Teflon coating. It provides effortless release. Eggs, starches, and burnt-on foods lift right off her surface. Plus, you can use metal utensils and not scratch her).

As for Fraser, it's best to see his movies only when he's starring as a Jay Ward cartoon character. I look forward to seeing him take a star turn in the upcoming *Hoppity Hooper,* with himself as Hooper, Rupert Everett as Professor Waldo Wigglesworth, and Kristin Scott Thomas as Susan Swivelhips.

THE LAST DAYS OF DISCO

Disco: surely the most influential cultural movement in the history of the world. The Enlighten-
ment? Not even close. The Renaissance and humanism?
No. In fact, eat me, humanism—you're so far off. Disco
has shaped the way we drink, eat, dance, make music,
wear feather boas, dress as Rosalind Russell, and consume
snack bags full of cocaine. For a brief time in the mid-
1970s, when "Disco Duck" ruled the charts, the sun did
not set on Rick Dees's kingdom. There are those who
would sacrifice the dearest thing they owned—their lives,
their very souls—just to shake it in the general vicinity of
Margaux Hemingway while "I'm Coming Out" thumped
loudly in their chests. Men of power subjugated themselves to the mighty gods of disco. Hamilton Jordan and
Henry Kissinger could be seen playfully bumping their
buttocks together, while model Beverly Johnson mock-
spanked them.

It had to end, of course. An empire that mighty is
doomed to conquer itself. Decades have passed since
disco's halcyon days. There are as many as four Diana Ross

face-lifts between that golden time and the present, and though the mirror balls are dusty and tarnished, and the light-up dance floor panels are, I don't know, disassembled and sold to an electronic parts firm out of Connecticut, the impact of disco is still being felt. Disco rereleases clog the market; silly, synthetic pants outsell sugar and pork bellies; more than eight hundred movies with campy disco themes were released last week alone.

One such film, Whit Stillman's effort *The Last Days of Disco,* is an encomium to that happier time. Happier, that is, if you are Gloria Gaynor, a Bee Gee, or Liza Minnelli. If you are none of these, your life now is almost assuredly happier, more productive, and Leo Sayer–free. *Disco* tells its story in the unmistakable Stillman style: Characters "say" stuff to each other while nothing really "happens."

As the film opens, it is 1980, and the two main characters, roommates Alice and Charlotte, go about this process of saying things to each other on their way to the most exclusive nightclub in Manhattan, perhaps the most exclusive in all of the boroughs. Charlotte is a brazen go-getter, while Alice is meek and kind. I think. It's difficult to pick up any clues from their acting, as it would appear that Stillman directed them to behave as though they were just given a large dose of horse tranquilizers. Alice stares at Charlotte through hooded eyes while Charlotte delivers her lines in the style of a Chili's waitress reciting the beer menu.

The club is a strange, cardboard world that resembles a soap opera set with all the life sucked out of it. Shirtless guys with Nazi hats flirt with other men wearing leather masks or harlequin outfits—it looks like one of Malcolm Forbes's garden parties. I question Stillman's choice of making disco enthusiasts appear even creepier than they actually are. One of the creeps, Tom (Robert Sean Leonard), picks up Alice and, after a brief flirtation, gives her a venereal disease. Or rather, they couple and, as a result, she *contracts* a venereal disease. He didn't just walk up and *hand* her a venereal disease. It's all rather unpleasant, and yet not unexpected given all the Donna Summer music these people take in. Charlotte pairs off with Jimmy, a wan advertising guy who talks like a full-grown *Peanuts* character, and Jennifer Beals makes a scary appearance as a woman who yells a lot. I mean, I know she's a maniac, maniac, but she was yelling like she had never yelled before.

A correction: One of the characters makes the claim that theirs is the greatest club the world has ever known. Anyone who's been to Dibbo's in Hudson, Wisconsin, knows this is just not the case.

The big problem with *The Last Days of Disco* is the strange, stilted tone that permeates every frame. The characters all seem like they'd been buried in the Pet Sematary and returned, undead. Their frequent quoting of J. D. Salinger only makes them seem more dead. It's a bizarre method of satirizing a group of people recognizable only to the eight people being satirized, though it gives me hope for my as yet unproduced film, which satirizes my old roommate Calvin. It's a scathing indictment that focuses on Calvin's annoying habit of using our hot pot to cook noodles in.

It is my hope that we can be done with this silly disco thing so that we might focus our attention on something of lasting value, like Jewel songs or Internet auction sites.

ISHTAR/ WATERWORLD

It is a widely held belief that King Richard III of England was as cruel and despotic as Shakespeare's depiction of him. But historians now believe that a smear campaign was launched against the man by a rival family, and letters from that time are surfacing, some stating "methinks he's not that bad" and that he's "not much to look at, but he's always been nice to thee." And though he may even have strangled the two young princes in the Tower of London, it turns out that the children were "annoying" and had "called him 'Uncle Humpback' " on several occasions. Surely more than one Plantagenet surreptitiously clapped him on the back with a, "Thank you. We all wanted to, but you had the guts."

The point is, once something gets in the public consciousness, it's hard to dislodge it. So it is with the belief that *Ishtar* and *Waterworld,* because of their abysmal box office performances, are just plain bad movies. Not true. They are *pretty darn bad* and *exceptionally* bad movies, respectively.

Ishtar is the story of two hard-luck songwriters who take

a job in Morocco and become entwined in a plot to overthrow the despotic ruler of Ishtar. Though it has some laughs, mostly what it does is plod. I know cognitively that it lasts only a couple hours, but I could swear that while I was watching it, evolution went to work and certain species of birds lost organs that had once been used to digest a long-dead food source. Oceans heaved, and continents shifted. The civilization I had known was reduced to a bump in the sand, just a speck in a huge, unrecognizable wasteland ruled by bearlike creatures that had moved down from the North and adapted to the desert atmosphere by eating hundreds of pounds of cicadas every day.

The truth is, *Ishtar* isn't the worst movie ever made. Some of the songs in it are quite funny, and it has a certain charm. It's better than *It's Pat: The Movie,* and almost as good as the second game of a doubleheader featuring the Twins and the Royals—somewhere in that general entertainment area.

Waterworld (sometimes referred to as *Fishtar* or *Kevin's Gate*) is a fine kettle of fish that never disappoints with its incompetence. Kevin Costner stars as Gorton of Gloucester, and Jeanne Tripplehorn as Mrs. Paul, in a futuristic tale that takes place after the polar ice caps have melted. Annoying men who sound like Popeye (the Smokers, because you see, they smoke cigarettes) chase after the hateful, misogynist Costner on jet-skis. One need only go to the Wisconsin Dells to see annoying men on jet-skis. I could have made the movie for the price of film and a couple of tickets to Tommy Bartlett's Water Show.

Dennis Hopper is the leader of the Smokers, and with every frame convinces me that someone has got to take his pot away. He's got to be over fifty, and that's just too old to be inhabiting the resiny world of "pinch hits" and "the munchies." He probably still laughs every time he thinks of Cheech and Chong doing their classic "Dave's not here, man" routine. Soon he'll be over at McCartney's house, stuffing towels under the door and listening to old *Head East* albums.

Waterworld is not good. It will make you headachey. If you must watch it, wait until an hour after eating. Wear polarized glasses, and use a high SPF sunscreen. No shoving or horseplay.

Before you go around spreading the bad news about a film, take an evening. Close the shades. Turn down the company of good friends. Shut that annoying book. Get into your boxer shorts or torn housecoat. Don't answer the phone. Eat a whole pizza right off the couch cushions. Pop in *Hello Again,* with Shelly Long and Corbin Bernsen. There. Ahhhhhh.

SPRING BREAK

Ask a handful of people where they were when Kennedy was shot, and you're likely to get a capsule view of a more innocent time, a peek into the hearts and minds of a generation who held on to the slender stem of hope even as the rose of peace was ripped from their tenuous grasp.

Ask a sample group from my generation where they were when they first saw *Spring Break,* and you're likely to get a similar view into a beerier time, when the slender neck of a Miller High Life was ripped from their stuporous grasp by Smitty, Murph, or Monster. You see, *Spring Break* meant a lot to us, and there are few who can't remember where they were when they first saw it. Except those who were drunk. So really, quite a few people won't remember where they were when they first saw it. But that doesn't diminish its impact.

It's important to set *Spring Break* in the proper context of history. The year was 1983, the drive-in was all but dead, and a young man named Corey Hart was dreaming up a little song about a handsome young man who "wore his sunglasses at night" so he could, so he could "keep track of the visions in his dreams." 'Twas a fecund time for Steve Perry and Journey, not to mention Rockwell, Duran Duran, *and* Patty Smyth, who was doing her damnedest to "shoot down the walls of heartache, bang bang." You see, "she was the warrior." The time was ripe for a film that dared to be shockingly stupid and brazenly puerile. There was no Pauly Shore—the hirsute doper was years away from forcing his powerful, shrewish mother to give him a film career. In steps *Spring Break,* a bold and powerful portrayal of the bacchanalia that takes place at Fort Lauderdale every year, and it becomes an instant smash, propelling the rite of spring break into the public consciousness. Pathetically, it was the *The Harder They Come* of my time.

The film made a huge impact on me, turning me away from the worthless study of music theory with a special emphasis on piano performance and toward a fruitful career of beery shenanigans. I've always been especially compelled by *Break*'s clear references to the commedia dell'arte and the stock characters therein. For *Spring Break,* like no other beach film before it, used a boilerplate approach to characters that was duplicated time and time again in the '80s with such films as *Revenge of the Nerds, Hot Dog . . . The Movie,* and *Hot Chili.*

These films' dramatic centers always revolve around an ingenue and her lover and their inability to have sex. The harlequins, Pierrots, and other zanni (in commedia, the comic servants) translate to be nerdy tape-spectacled losers; greedy, overbearing relatives; cagey upperclassmen who would lead the ingenues astray; and, my favorite, the indefatigable party animal who can crush beer cans on his head/open beer bottles with his teeth/has a dog trained to take off women's tops, etc.

With these stock characters in place, a director of the '80s could pick his setting—say, a hotel that hires young summer help—audition some hopeful actors and, in the course of two weeks' principal photography and a week of additional dialogue replacement, crush their souls and get a direct-to-video winner out of the deal, quick as you please. It was a system that worked. But it barely lasted the decade.

I believe now that the round table of our Camelot-in-Lauderdale is split asunder, and like Kennedy, our heroes have faded into time. The cast of *Break* . . . are gone. Sean S. Cunningham, as far as anyone knows, he never made another movie. David Knell, he never made another movie. Steve Basset, he never made another movie. Perry Lang, he never made another . . . well, you get the idea.

The legacy they left behind is a tenuous one. A legacy that is sticky with dried Schlitz Malt Liquor. The bad sex jokes echo off the walls and reappear in Chris Farley or David Spade movies. Or Chris Farley–David Spade movies. Or Adam Sandler movies. Or Adam Sandler–Chris Farley–David Spade movies. And they sound hollow.

Me, well, I sit in my basement, laughing loudly at the few tapes I've managed to collect from that glorious time. I nose about the video stores, hoping for a laserdisc remastering of *Assault of the Party Nerds*, or *Hot Moves*. I still call Smitty and Murph, ask them to come over and watch my slow-play SVHS recordings of *Student Affairs* and *Off the Mark*. But they beg off, citing families and careers. Smitty claims never to have met me, and Murph always whines about his job as Cook County Assistant D.A.

PART NINE

MEGA-MEGACHEESE

THE BLAIR WITCH PROJECT

Everyone agrees: *The Blair Witch Project* is the most exciting entertainment event since The Alan Parsons Project. Shot on a budget of just over four dollars, the film is expected to make eight hundred jillion dollars worldwide, with several hundred kajillion more expected from sales of *Blair Witch* fanny packs. In an unprecedented move, the government allowed the PR department for *Blair Witch* to have control of all television, radio, and print, President Clinton himself stating, "It is a matter of national entertainment." Internet promotions for the film were also very successful, with www.blairwitch.com getting more hits than www.slimwhitman.com and the Isuzu Amigo 1999 Engine Specification sites combined.

Until it went into wide release, false rumors about the film were propagated, among them that the documentary footage was the actual recording of a real event. A few claimed to have had heard that it was some sort of hippie, Wiccan commune. The most widely circulated was that *Blair Witch Project* was a comedy inspired by the character Blair from the hit TV series *The Facts of Life*. That rumor had Mrs. Garrett and Tootie going deep into the woods to look for Natalie, who, according to legends from the surrounding communities, refused to help Blair with her homework.

I was busy and unable to see *Blair Witch* its first few weeks in the theater until finally an Artisan Entertainment executive showed up at my door with a court order, and I was forced to go. From the very first frame, I was overcome by a feeling of suffocating dread, because the large man in the seat next to me had spread-eagled his legs and didn't seem to mind that about 8 percent of his body surface was in contact with about 25 percent of mine. Onscreen, Josh, Mike, and Heather, amateur filmmakers, were gathering footage for a documentary about the legend of a witch who supposedly haunts the woods near Burkittsville, Maryland. She's called the Blair Witch because the town was formerly named Blair. Because there is also a Blair County, Pennsylvania, some of the more punctilious locals refer to her as The Burkittsville, Maryland (Formerly Blair, Maryland) Witch. The witch feels that this undercuts her potential to frighten, and in an attempt to cement the scarier "Blair Witch" name, leaves little stick figures bearing the message "Blair Witch Available for Hire" on people's doorsteps.

The crew interviews the local "crazy woman" who claims to have had an encounter with the witch. According to her, the witch floated up to her as she sat alone by a stream and opened her robe, revealing coarse hair all over her body. Obviously a cry for help from a women in very serious need of depilatory. A fisherman also claims to have seen the ghostly form of a woman rise out of the water and hover there, though when pressed, he admits it might have been a rock bass. Armed with the knowledge that the witch is as hairy as Robin Williams, they head off into the woods to investigate.

Three minutes in, they get lost and decide to set up camp for the night, even though it's 9:00 A.M. They are awakened by strange sounds—squeals and eerie pounding noises. It's just the witch tinkering with the exhaust system on her '74 AMC Javelin. She felt she had to move deep into the woods when neighbors complained that she regularly ran her radial sander after ten o'clock. The frightened campers awake to find several small piles of stones left near their tent. It is, of course, the witch version of the pineapple, a sign of hospitality. The witch grows angry when they don't even send her the traditional dried rabbit offal as thanks.

As they become more lost (if it's even possible to become "more" lost. I suppose it's not really a matter of degree. You can't *not* know where you are more or less than you currently do), they grow more desperate and wonder if they just shouldn't start eating each other now. They camp another night, and the witch, trying one more time to be hospitable, spreads slime on Josh's backpack. While doing this, she trips on a stump and lands atop their tent. They are understandably alarmed, and when they begin shouting and screaming, the witch runs away, embarrassed that she came at all. Josh doesn't like the slime on his bag, which further hurts the witch's feelings. It's a big misunderstanding that could have easily been rectified had not everyone overreacted.

Now the witch is forced to kidnap the ungrateful Josh,

leaving Heather and Mike completely Josh-less. They search for him, following the distant sound of his voice, but since they couldn't find their way out of a phone booth, they come up short finding him as well. The witch leaves a helpful clue: Some of Josh's body parts tied in a cloth and wrapped in a bundle of sticks. Clearly the witch could use some gifts bags and decorative tissue paper (a nice present for her next birthday, perhaps?). Josh's trail eventually leads to a dilapidated house in the woods (my friend observed: Why not just follow the driveway out to the road?). They follow his voice upstairs first, then down, where both of them hit their head on a low ceiling beam, and the movie ends.

When it was over, the crowd was completely silent, wondering if perhaps The Project's funding was cut.

I was almost ready to believe the *Blair Witch* hype: "It does for camping what *Jaws* did for going to the beach." Then I remembered, *Jaws* never made me afraid to go to the beach, because I grew up in Illinois. There are very few saltwater beaches in Illinois, even fewer that are infested with sharks. Besides, not going camping is always a good idea. *Blair Witch* doesn't make camping out any more or less horrible. Deer ticks and sandburrs are what prevent me from going camping, not hairy witches.

One comment I heard from more than one *Blair Witch* viewer was, "It didn't really scare me at the time, but it scared me later when I'd had a chance to think about it." I guess people left the cold, dark theater and in the bright light of day decided that it was rational to fear evisceration at the hands of a nocturnal murderous witch.

The Blair Witch Project is kind of a cross between *Southern Comfort* and *Hansel and Gretel*. Its ability to frighten is largely related to the watcher's worldview and whether or not it allows for hirsute killer witches.

Personally, I keep my oven running at all times just in case she pays a visit.

MYSTERY SCIENCE THEATER 3000: THE MOVIE

In 1996, I was involved in making *Mystery Science Theater 3000: The Movie*. In the spirit of fairness, it was suggested that I critique it as I would any other film. I tried to forget the fact that I had anything to do with its making, and just watch it as another viewer. The method I used was to drink eight Black and Tans in just under twenty-four minutes; with any luck, this would erase the memory of my own involvement. Here's my review.

Miyitry sInce THEATTTRE 3000, the mvoe? Wths Robot all abut? Ths kind of funny. Whos that guy?
TTTTTTTTTTTTTTTTTTTTTTTTTTTTTTTTTTTTTTTTTTTTT
TTTTTTTTTTTTTTTTTTTTTTTTTTTTTTTTTTTTTTTTTTTTT
TTTTTTTTTTTTTTTTTTTTTTTTTTTTTTTTTTTTTTTTTTTTT
TTTTTTTTTTTTTTTTTTT . . .

And then there are 423 pages of Ts, because I fell asleep on the keyboard. I abandoned that method and just went ahead with my review.

Mystery Science Theater 3000: The Movie is the big-screen version of the television show *Mystery Science Theater 3000: The Television Show.* The show was created in 1988 for a small station in Minneapolis to fill a need for more "plastic puppet-based entertainment." The concept was the result of extensive market research and in its first incarnation featured an old Swiss woman, a fir tree, and a smoked ham making fun of Lyle Waggoner infomercials. Test audiences were enthusiastic and especially loved the fir tree, but they felt that the smoked ham was "too southern." Seizing on this, the producers ditched the smoked ham, replacing it with *McMillan & Wife*'s John Schuck. The fir tree's part was beefed up and given to Erin Gray in her first role as a tree. The show tanked and was retooled again to include a guy and two robots making fun of B-movies. The characters would take breaks and put on "skits" or "playlets" in an attempt to amuse, or possibly just irritate.

The film follows the same basic formula as the television show, except that you have to pay for it. Dr. Clayton Forrester, a mad scientist, has trapped a man in space and forces him to watch the Rex Reason film *This Island Earth*, the story of an alien invasion by supertan aliens with large foreheads who look like Charlie Rich. It's funny enough, if you like that sort of thing, but it shouldn't prevent you from doing other things like changing your vacuum cleaner bag or bleeding your water heater.

It should be noted that the film is only seventy-three minutes long, shorter than the television show, which ran two hours with Jolly Rancher commercials, ninety-five minutes without. As far as movie value goes, you'd be better of with *Reds, Lawrence of Arabia,* or even *Gremlins 2: The New Batch,* which runs 107 minutes. At $7.00 a ticket, that amounts to 6.5 cents a minute, a substantial savings over the pricier *MST*'s 9.6 cents a minute. For a real value, try the uncut version of *Greed.* It's eight hours long, which is under a penny and half a minute. You may have to fly to Germany to see it, however, so you should figure airfare, lodging, and sausage into that price.

As a movie that relies heavily on puppets, *Mystery Science Theater 3000: The Movie* isn't too bad, although I'd rank it behind *Puppet Master* and perhaps *Puppet Master 2.* Now that I think of it, *Puppet Master 3: Toulon's Revenge* has a bit more going for it. *Puppet Master 4* kept the series alive pretty well, and you know what, *Puppet Master 5: The Final Chapter* comes out on top as well. Rent *MST3K:TM* only if those and *The Thunderbirds* series are all checked out.